LEO ROBITSCHEK

THE NOMAD COCKTAIL BOOK

Illustrations by Antoine Ricardou

TEN SPEED PRESS
California | New York

CONTENTS

PREFACE
by Will Guidara

Greetings, dear reader. Although you don't know it yet, you're about to get Leo'd, and I couldn't be happier for you.

What? You don't know what that means? Don't worry, you haven't missed the latest pop-culture trend or internet meme. *Getting Leo'd* is a phrase we use at Make It Nice, the company that comprises our restaurants and bars: Eleven Madison Park, The NoMad, The NoMad Bar, and Made Nice. In its purest form, it describes the following. Once in a while, one of us or a member of our team will show up to work bleary-eyed and disheveled, which is neither normal nor acceptable in the organization. Inevitably, the shorthand explanation for this sorry and hilarious sight is, "I got Leo'd last night."

The phrase guarantees instant forgiveness for having been out later than is prudent, after our kick-ass bar director Leo Robitschek spontaneously treated us to a magical night spent bouncing from one favorite haunt to another, until we realized—much too late—that time had breezed by. The forgiveness comes because Leo is a force of nature, as irresistible in his ability to sweep people up for an evening of harmless revelry as he is at inspiring his army of mixologists to help redefine cocktail culture in the United States.

I am writing this preface at the bar at The NoMad in New York City. There are few places I'd rather savor a drink than at the bar in one of our restaurants. That's not a brag; it's a compliment and tribute to Leo. I used to have a predisposition toward Italian reds, but am now savoring what has become my go-to cocktail: a Manhattan. The drink—fashioned from whiskey or rye, vermouth, and a dash of bitters—is a lot like Leo: simple, straightforward, and perfectly crafted. (I'd be less than honest if I didn't also acknowledge that, like a Manhattan, Leo can get you hammered.)

The best restaurants are extensions and expressions of their creators, and the same is true of bars. And our bars, from the sophisticated elegance of Eleven Madison Park to the posh playpen of the NoMads, grew from the knowledge, passion, taste, and teachings of Leo. So who is this Mr. Robitschek? Well, that's a sticky question because he's actually two people. The first, the one whom guests and lucky diners know, is an affable, twenty-first-century iteration of the quintessential American barman—hair cropped close like Clark Kent's, silk vest or smoking jacket draped over a well-starched collared shirt, arms that somehow never tire of shaking or stirring, and a smile that conveys rakish charm.

Similar to our bars, which make you feel as though you are at the center of the modern cocktail universe while at the same time transported to its golden age, Leo is a man a bit out of time. Had he lived in the mid- to late-nineteenth century, when the lion's share of classic cocktails was first devised, I imagine that he'd have concocted his own hall of famers to stand tin to tin with the Old-Fashioned, Gin Fizz, Mint Julep, and other greats. In fact, the future may show that he has actually done this, by creating countless contemporary drinks that steer clear of the pyrotechnics and shock value (outlandish glassware, dry ice) that have seduced his contemporaries. As the decades, and then the centuries, blur together, perhaps Leo's Hot Lips (jalapeño-infused blanco tequila, mezcal, pineapple, and vanilla) and his Start Me Up (bourbon, Trinidadian rum, Strega, orange bitters, honey, ginger, and lemon) *will* be named in the same breath as the cocktails that preceded them; they're already being ordered together. All of which is a long way of saying that Leo is a living, breathing example of substance over style. Not that Leo is a slave to the past. In reality, he's a quietly intense innovator. Beyond his signature drinks, one of his singular contributions to cocktail culture is his systematization of craft cocktails at the level and volume our restaurants demand. The fast-food industry had Ray Kroc; the auto industry had Henry Ford; we have Leo Robitschek.

Like most creatives who want to accomplish Big Things, Leo knows the force and inevitability of collaboration and empowerment. His recipe-testing sessions rank as legend within the industry. Periodically, he gathers several team members from one restaurant to dream up new cocktails en masse—mixing, tasting, debating, and re-testing while he himself bangs away at his laptop like Stevie Wonder at full tilt, capturing every detail. I say "from one restaurant" because Leo has concocted different and constantly changing drink lists for *all* of our venues, including three different NoMads (New York, Los Angeles, Las Vegas), that each reflect the distinct character of their environs.

The second Leo persona is a private yang that balances his public yin. We, his professional family, have a backstage pass to the mad scientist who's driven to extremes by seriousness about his work, a love for the company, and a deep and instinctive sense of hospitality. If he spots a guest looking lost, he's the first one to offer help, but his passion can also express itself in, let's say, "more intense" ways. Like many geniuses, if somebody doesn't hew to his vision, he will let them know. He also has a full complement of absent-minded-professor tics, functions on his own schedule and priorities, and is constantly in motion, whether from place to place, idea to idea, or side to side as he stands and sways during conversations and meetings. Can he be difficult? Of course, he can. But so can the rest of us. And his quirks come from the same place as ours—not serving an ego but rather the greater good, meaning, our company, our team, our restaurants, our bars, and—above all—our guests. We love *both* sides of this true original and indispensable colleague.

Two of Leo's greatest passions are sharing his knowledge and his enthusiasm. Unsurprisingly, he drafted his team to help with this book, giving them another way to participate, another outlet for *their* own passions, and another thing to be proud of achieving together. But perhaps nothing sums up Leo more than a funny historical footnote about this book. (Well, it's funny to me but a lingering grudge for him, and something that tells you all you need to know about his single-minded commitment to craftsmanship, detail, and perfection.) He wanted desperately to include ten more pages . . . about *ice.*

If you're curious what those pages might have taught you and you happen to see Leo at one of our bars, by all means, ask him. He'll be only too happy to tell you. You might be there for a while. But then you'll be able to tell people one of the greatest things any of us can tell anybody—that you *got Leo'd.*

Happy reading, and cheers!

FOREWORD
by David Wondrich

We all have our little time-travel fantasies. Ever since I started digging into the annals of the cocktail, my particular E-ticket daydream has involved popping back to, say, 1893 and strolling up the stretch of Broadway between Twenty-Third Street and Thirty-Fourth Street, with (the point of the exercise) stops at all the hotels. At the end of the nineteenth century, New York hotel bars had the most elegant décor, the finest liquors, the most skillful bartenders, and the sportiest, most interesting clientele in the world; and that stretch of Broadway—the so-called "cocktail route"—had most of the grand hotels.

I'd start my walk by going half a block up the street and making a sharp left through the doors of the Fifth Avenue Hotel, at the northwest corner of Twenty-Third Street and Broadway. The Fifth Avenue was the sort of place where princes and presidents stayed; where power was wielded and political careers were launched with a quiet handshake. But while Jim Gray, the hotel's longtime head bartender, was known for sporting two or three different elaborate and colorfully embroidered silk vests during the course of a shift, his drinks were anything but fancy. His signature drink was an Old-Fashioned Whiskey Cocktail so down-to-earth that he didn't even use bitters in it. He served up the first one to Ulysses S. Grant in 1881 (or so he claimed), and I'd have him mix one for me, too.

Then, as much as I'd like to linger, I'd make the long trek up to Broadway and Twenty-Fourth, where I'd call in at the quiet, tony Hotel Albemarle and persuade James Burri, the Swiss bartender, to make me a gin-and-raspberry Albemarle Fizz. After that, I'd need a bit of a walk, so I'd cut across Madison Square and put in at the old Ashland House on Twenty-Fourth Street, a block east of the park. In 1933, Patsy Duffy, the head bartender, would write the Repeal Era's definitive bar guide. In 1893, he was still a genial young emigrant from County Roscommon who claimed to make a fine Irish Whiskey Punch. I'd find out. I'd want to stay a spell, I'm sure. But up next would be the Hoffman House, at the corner of Twenty-Fifth and Broadway, and its bar.

And what a bar it was: opulent, even decadent, it was a symphony in carved mahogany, brass, and painted pink female flesh. But it was also excellent—under the direction of owner Edward S. Stokes and head bartender Billy Mulhall, it was widely held to mix the best drinks in the country. But what to have? A Peerless Cocktail, a New Amsterdam, a Hoffman House Special? A Mountain Dew Sour? A Northrop Fizz? A Billy Deutsch? One of the six different Toddies or five Coolers that Mulhall's list advertised? Then again, old-time bartenders prided themselves on their ability to size up a customer and fit him out with something appropriate, so why not trust myself to Mulhall's judgment?

If I could pry myself away from the Hoffman House and weave my way up to Twenty-Sixth Street, I could catch my breath with a Gin Rickey at the bar where it was introduced to the city, at the St. James Hotel on the west, or "dollar" side, of Broadway. Or I could cross to the east, or "shilling" side, and have a Delmonico Cocktail at the bar of Delmonico's famous restaurant. At either, I'd find a lively crowd of the rich and sporty; probably best to check 'em both out. If I were to continue east on Twenty-Sixth, I'd hit the Brunswick House, whose bar was a bastion of the country gentry, and . . . at this point I should just stick to Broadway, particularly since Twenty-Seventh Street and Twenty-Eighth Street formed a Scylla and Charybdis of, respectively, "parlor houses"—brothels—and gambling dens, and I'm not the type to patronize either (and if I were I certainly wouldn't admit it here). Even if I dodged those I'd probably find myself stuck on Fifth Avenue, beguiled by the bar of the Holland House Hotel or the Manhattan Club or the brand-new Waldorf Hotel. I might never find my way back to Broadway.

That would mean I'd miss Jim Butler at the Gilsey House, at the northeast corner of Broadway and Twenty-Ninth Street, and the opportunity to sip one of his Florence Cocktails while watching him water the mixed throng of ward-heelers, sports, and actors who patronized the joint (and went through fifty-two dozen lemons a day). I wouldn't want to do that. Nor would I want to pass up the chance to pause for a moment in front of the Bijou Theatre, on the dollar side just above Thirtieth Street, where the great pioneer of American bartending Jerry Thomas had his "Museum and Art Gallery" back in the 1870s. By this point, even a daydreamer has to acknowledge the effect of all those drinks; I'd most likely, therefore, skip the dubious pleasures of Dick Darling's rough and ready saloon and the massive White Horse billiard hall, both on that stretch of Broadway, and head straight for the Grand Hotel at the southeast corner of Thirty-First Street for one of its famous Vermouth Cocktails (surely that couldn't do me any harm). And perhaps I'd merely poke my head in at the bar of the Hotel Imperial, up at Thirty-Second Street, to look at the large paintings of "scenes from poems by American poets" with which it was adorned. Okay, if John Palmer's behind the bar I'd better have one of his gin-and-vermouth Imperial Cocktails. But that's *it*.

By the time Prohibition came in 1919, most of these bars were gone. The hotel district had moved above Forty-Second Street, as had Delmonico's, and many of the survivors were torn down to be replaced by commercial lofts. Of them all, only the Gilsey House, the Imperial, and the Holland House are even still standing, though not as hotels. The neighborhood became a place for light manufacturing, wholesaling, and peddling, not drinking, carousing, and carrying on. At the end of the twentieth century it saw a bit of a revival as those loft buildings proved useful spaces for dance clubs and such, and the new century brought in a restaurant or two, but they didn't really change things much. The neighborhood still kept the ragtag daytime bustle and the nighttime darkness and silence that had characterized it for almost a century. There was nothing to recall its former glory; none of the snap and dash and great, gaudy show. There was no great cocktail bar anywhere on what should be hallowed ground for American bartending.

Enter The NoMad. Four years ago, I sat down with Daniel Humm, Will Guidara, and Leo Robitschek of Eleven Madison Park, the flagship for fine dining on the east side of Madison Square. We were at the beer garden on the roof of Eataly, which was fitting: Eataly is on the site of the Fifth Avenue Hotel. What they outlined for me was a plan to build a hotel bar that could hold its head up in that kind of company. It would be at Broadway and Twenty-Eighth, in a fine old office building right in the middle of the old cocktail route, and Leo would be its Billy Mulhall. I was intrigued, to be sure; if anybody could pull it off, it was Leo. Then, a few months later, I walked into the bar.

My first reaction, frankly, was to laugh. Dominick Venegas was behind the bar, backlit and standing between two pagan idol–size wooden elephants. Bearded, burly, and grinning, Dominick looked like the head priest of some dark cult of the cocktail. This was not the standard, could-be-anywhere New York hotel bar. It's as if Leo and his crew drilled deep into the bedrock beneath the building and found the pool of residual bar juju that had lurked there untapped for a hundred years. The drinks I had that night, and in fact every drink I've had at NoMad since, served to confirm that impression.

Now I don't have to dream of Jim Gray and John Palmer. I've got Leo Robitschek. And Chris Lowder and Jessica Gonzalez and Lacy Hawkins and Pietro Collina and—and I'll let Leo tell the rest. It's his story, after all, not mine.

INTRODUCTION

It's three o'clock in the morning and I'm sitting in New York City at our local bar with a few members of my team, reflecting over a few pints on that night's service. My day began seventeen hours earlier, at ten o'clock the previous morning—which alternately feels like it was moments ago and weeks in the past. When I walked through the door of The NoMad yesterday morning, the prep team had already been at it for hours, producing more than one hundred quarts of juice and the four hundred hand-cut citrus twists we would need for service that day. Bartenders and barbacks arrived next to ready the Elephant Bar and its sibling next door; there were infusions and syrups to prepare and inventory, tools to gather and work stations to set, cases and cases of liquor to receive and catalog.

It's a mad dash to prepare for service; over the course of a day, hundreds of guests will come through our doors. Some will dine in the restaurant, some will lounge in the library, some will pull up a stool to sit with us at the bars. Nearly all of them will have a cocktail. Our team consists of fifteen people per night, and everyone works their asses off during their ten-hour shifts—stirring, mixing, and serving nonstop. Now that it's 3 a.m. we should, admittedly, call it a night—because tomorrow, we do it all over again.

I began bartending at Eleven Madison Park (EMP) in the spring of 2005. At that time, the restaurant was a busy brasserie known for its warm service and accessible fare. The bar was a meeting place for local businesspeople and a holding area for guests waiting for a table. The cocktail menu comprised eight proprietary drinks unchanged since the restaurant's opening in 1998. The bartenders were all friendly and efficient; they were as thrilled to pour you a glass of wine or fashion you a gin and tonic as to mix one of the drinks from the menu. But, as with most dining destinations in New York in 2005, the restaurant had no real cocktail culture.

In 2006, EMP began to evolve. A rising chef, Daniel Humm, took the helm of the kitchen, and a young dining room guy, Will Guidara, joined the team as our general manager. They were determined to make radical changes to the restaurant—to elevate the experience to a level worthy of the luxurious grandeur of its dining room.

As always, with change came resistance. Many of the staff had worked there for years. There were some who embraced this new direction—but for those who did *not*, well, their tenure at the restaurant was drawing to a close. So I was scared shitless when Will and Daniel called me into their office for a talk. I was anxiously expecting the boot, but I was wrong. They had very high aspirations for the bar at EMP, and they felt that I, acting as head bartender, was the person to take it there. They made their goal explicit: They wanted our bar—in spite of the fact that it was a "restaurant bar"—to be one of the best in the world.

In 2006, good cocktails were not associated with restaurants, let alone fine dining restaurants. There were a few pioneering cocktail bars, like Pegu Club and Milk and Honey, that were bringing back the craft of the cocktail and devoting themselves to techniques and ingredients just as chefs did. But for the most part, you would be hard-pressed to find innovative and well-made cocktails at many other bars, let alone restaurant bars.

Essentially, Will and Chef were asking me to do something that had never been done before: create a cocktail program that maintained the rigorous standards of a top-tier fine dining restaurant—drinks that weren't just an afterthought, but expressed the spirit and philosophy of the restaurant in which they were served. It might have been my lack of confidence, or maybe my shock that I was still gainfully employed, but my first reaction was to laugh out loud. This was *not* the response they'd wanted to hear. That's when I received the first of many "Will Guidara" looks. (Years later, Will admitted that he thought about letting me go, right there and then.)

I not only survived the rest of the meeting, but I also started to become very, very excited by the ideas Will and Chef were sharing. Over the course of the next two hours, we ironed out our goals. We wanted to create a four-star restaurant for *our* generation, one that didn't focus solely on food and wine, but rather approached everything we served—beer, coffee, tea, and what was to become the focus of my life, cocktails—with the same intensity of purpose.

When I left their office and stepped back behind the bar at EMP, I looked at it in a way that I never had before. I couldn't help but think about where I was four years earlier: sitting behind a desk at an investment bank. It was a good job, I was making decent money, and above all else, my mom was proud. But I hated it. After a year of trying to convince myself that this was what I wanted to do, I finally quit, officially beginning my quarter-life crisis. A friend of mine was an investor at the very popular restaurant Sushi Samba, and suggested I work there. So a few weeks later, I traded in my suit for a brightly colored shirt and tight black pants, and got to work behind the bar. Sushi Samba was one of the hippest places in town—it even made multiple appearances on *Sex and the City*. (The show filmed at EMP a few years later—remember the scene when Carrie found out Big was engaged and knocked over a tray while tripping down the stairs? To this day I question why they were so enamored with me and the restaurants where I was working. But I digress. . . .) The training at Sushi Samba was intense. They required mandatory wine, sake, beer, and spirit classes, which were led by Paul Tanguay and his staff. The classes opened my eyes to the vast world of beverage, and I slowly began to appreciate in ways I never had before the things I had been serving. But my appreciation for well-crafted cocktails didn't come until a few months later when a coworker took me to the new hot spot, Pegu Club.

It was a Wednesday at 11 p.m. when we walked into the bar. I opened the menu to see a list of unfamiliar cocktails, all of which included ingredients I had never seen. I wanted a vodka cocktail and the only one they had contained a smoky Scotch that sounded absolutely disgusting to me at the time. Maybe the bartender overheard my desire for vodka, or perhaps he saw my look of confusion, but he suggested I order a Gin-Gin Mule. I did, hesitantly. Unsure of what to expect, I glanced over at the bar while he was making my drink, and I was captivated. The process was beautiful, almost like a dance—it was clear he took his craft seriously. The way he measured every ingredient precisely using this thing that I would later learn to call a *jigger*; the way he hit the mint, bunched it together, and placed it perfectly in the drink, effortlessly but with absolute intention. I was fascinated. And then the first sip. It was so flavorful—spice from the ginger, a minty freshness, a citrus bang, and gin, combined in the most pleasant way imaginable. Had I *really* just enjoyed gin?

Back in the real world of my day job, I still wasn't even sure that being a bartender was my true calling. I'd always wanted to be a doctor, but years earlier had given up on the idea because I never thought I'd be able to afford medical school. But working in restaurants in New York City, I came to realize that there was no limit to how much debt one person could be in, so I took out some more student loans in order to pursue my dream. I enrolled in the pre-med post-baccalaureate program at Hunter College and began my studies while continuing to bartend at night. Trying to juggle school, work, and life was almost unmanageable at first—homework, so much fucking homework!—until I applied for a job at one of Danny Meyer's properties, EMP. Many of my friends had gone to work for Danny, and said he was running restaurants in a different, more respectful way. They were happy and had balanced lives; mine was full of stress and chaos. When I was offered a position tending bar at EMP, I accepted without hesitation.

Flash forward one year, and there I was, behind the bar at EMP after my meeting with Will and Chef, who had just presented me with the largest challenge of my career. You can appreciate why I was a bit overwhelmed. But I knew how I'd start. My feeling is that any time you are trying to build something from the ground up, you have to start with the basics. So the first revamped cocktail menu at EMP featured a list of classic ones I had been making at home since that first night at Pegu Club: Bronx Cocktail, Last Word, Sazerac, Ritz, Brandy Crusta, Paloma, Singapore Sling, and a Vodka Negroni (gasp!). It turned out that this list of classics ended up being one of the secrets of our success—our team focused on perfecting each drink on our rather small menu. Guests were excited to discover these historic recipes, and they began to realize drinks really *do* taste better when they're treated with precision. Even the G&T boys from Credit Suisse (not known for being the most adventurous diners at EMP) started to get excited about the new drinks.

One day, the next evolution of our bar program was sparked when I was working lunch service and a guest ordered an iced tea. We had recently created a seasonal syrup program for our iced teas, so when I placed the tea in front of him I put three different syrups alongside it: simple syrup, pomegranate hibiscus, and ginger lime. Upon naming each, I realized that our pastry team had been making two essential cocktail components—grenadine (which is essentially a pomegranate syrup) and the base of ginger beer—just a few feet from where I was standing. Up to this point, we were using purchased products, just like the majority of other bars in town, while on the other side of the wall we had all the tools to make, well, whatever we dreamed of. Recognizing that we could work with an entire team of talented chefs, with unbelievable palates and walk-ins full of exquisite ingredients, opened up a whole new realm of possibilities. Soon the pastry chefs became my best friends, and over the next several months we served cocktails using house-made orgeat; fresh syrups of raspberry, malted banana, spiced pumpkin; and more. We started brandying our own local cherries, created our first house bitters, and crafted a nonalcoholic cocktail around an heirloom tomato soda that Chef and I developed together. Now being a restaurant bar was no longer something that we needed to overcome; it was an advantage. This collaboration between the bar and the kitchen has defined our cocktail programs ever since.

From there we began working with the kitchen in other ways; not just to create elements for our drinks, but also looking to them for inspiration, whether from ingredients they were using or for the flavor combinations they were creating. One night, Chef presented a new dish at EMP, a roasted duck with lavender and honey, the only item on that EMP menu that is still served today. I was blown away when I first tasted its smoky, floral, gamey flavors, and I really wanted to re-create them in a cocktail. Combining smoky and floral notes may seem common now, but back then, it was game-changing. So the Bee Lavender (page 115) was born, one of the first cocktails I was really proud of, and one of many inspired by our kitchen.

One day in 2010, Will and Chef once again asked to meet with me in their office. And so I went, with no clue of what to expect, still a little bit scared, but much more confident. Will gave me a new look, a look that I had not seen before, but one that apparently meant "are you *sure* you want to be a doctor?"

This is the conversation that ensued.

Will: *What do you want to do with your life?*
Me: *I'm going to be a doctor.*
Will: *Are you* sure *you want to be a doctor?*
Me: *I just spent $60,000 on school; I'm going to be a doctor.*
Chef: *Let's pretend you can't be a doctor; then what would you want to be?*

Honestly, I'd asked myself the same question before. It was becoming very apparent—to me, to Will, and to everyone around me—that my love of cocktails wasn't just a passing interest. And we were all starting to question how I could just leave it behind. So when Chef asked me what I would do if I *wasn't* going to be a doctor, I knew the answer. After all, I had invested just as much time researching cocktails as I had spent preparing for medical school. I was in love with the history and folklore of cocktails and the story of the great hotel bars of the past (some of which still existed, though they had lost their luster). I would often find myself in a daze, designing *my* grand hotel bar—but how do you break it to your Venezuelan Jewish mother that you are foregoing medical school to be a bartender?

So I told Will and Chef (it sounds crazy, but I promise this is true) that if I wasn't going to be a doctor, I wanted to open a hotel bar. Will looked at me and said, "Let's go for a walk."

The three of us stepped out of EMP, went north, and walked across Madison Square Park. We took a left on Twenty-Sixth Street and a right on Broadway and walked up to the corner of Twenty-Eighth. We entered a boarded-up service area, rounded a few corners, and stood between two buildings surrounded by about fifteen feet of garbage covered in snow. Chef looked at me with a big smile and said, "Here it is!" It was, of course, the site of the future NoMad.

Two years later, in 2012, I found myself standing in the same place, this time on a Persian rug on top of a limestone floor, underneath a glass-ceilinged atrium, looking at *my* fully stocked mahogany bar. The last year had been insane; I was no longer in school, but I was busier than ever, my days and nights fully consumed with opening The NoMad. We were developing training manuals, hiring staff, ordering glassware, writing a spirits list, producing syrups, and, most time-consuming of all, developing a list of fifty cocktails that would be served throughout the entire hotel but come out of only one bar.

The entire process required an amazing team, and I was fortunate to have the best one could hope for. Our staff included people I had trained at EMP, others I had managed during the apprentice program at Tales of the Cocktail, and still others whose work I had admired while perched on stools in other bars throughout the city. These were the people who would allow Chef, Will, and me to follow through on our ambitious goal: to create a modern-day version of the grand hotel bars of the past.

March 26, 2012—opening day—arrived. We were ready. We had trained our staff extensively, prepared all our syrups and infusions, procured the best tools for the job, and created a list of tirelessly tested cocktails.

But things didn't go as planned. We opened the doors and we got *crushed*. Expecting to sell a couple of hundred cocktails, based on our experience at EMP, we sold more than a thousand on our first night. Yet we were still a restaurant bar, and guests wanted their cocktails within five minutes, or at the very least before their appetizer arrived—it seemed impossible. How were we going to make this many craft cocktails at such a high volume in such a short period of time? I thought to myself, "Maybe it would have been easier to be a doctor."

We couldn't compromise on the quality of our drinks, and I refused to rob our menu of the diversity I was so proud of, but we needed to make some kind of change. Once again, looking to the kitchen gave us our solution. We started to treat our prep just as the kitchen treats its mise en place: prepping all the ingredients in advance; incorporating flavors into syrups and infusions rather than adding them à la minute; and finding more efficient ways to set up our bar. I couldn't have survived without my team, and I continue to be amazed that in spite of fifteen- and sixteen-hour shifts we didn't lose any opening bar staff in the first year and a half.

In the time since writing the first version of this book, so much has happened. We won the 2014 James Beard Award for Outstanding Bar Program as well as numerous Tales of the Cocktail awards, including Best American Hotel Bar, Best American Restaurant Bar, Best High Volume Cocktail Bar, and Best American Bar Team. We also reached number three in The World's 50 Best Bars and won Best Bar in North America two years in a row. The NoMad has expanded to Los Angles, Las Vegas, and London; but, more important, we've built an incredible family and a strong culture and continue to grow and evolve our program every day.

The following pages tell the story of The NoMad through our cocktails. Our program continues to evolve in the pursuit of excellence, yet I am constantly reminded that my success is due not only to hard work, but also to timing and luck. I am grateful that I get to spend my life creating drinking experiences for so many different kinds of people, surrounded by an inspiring team (all of whom know how to shake better than me, and also have more tattoos). I am also happy to report that my Venezuelan Jewish mother is proud of her bartender son.

HOW TO USE
THIS BOOK

This book reflects my style of bartending, one that has developed through plenty of research along with lots of trial and error. I did not have a mentor coming up behind the bar, nor was I trained by one of the many great bar families. My cocktails are inspired by my surroundings, family and friends, books I've read, and the many talented people I've worked with over the years.

I've always been one to constantly question things, a trait I believe has served me well throughout my career, and just as I encourage my staff to have a voice, I urge you to get in touch should you need any help or have questions about the recipes in this book.

The recipes that follow have been tested extensively and served at our bars throughout The NoMad. Most of them can be quickly re-created at home, while others will require a few hours of prep work.

Every cocktail recipe is written in standard U.S. units—so, ounces, teaspoons, and the like—measurements that should be familiar to you and that we use to build our cocktails every single day. A section of basics, which includes syrups and infusions, follows the cocktail recipes. You will note that the ingredients in those recipes are expressed in metric units, which we find are more accurate for measuring larger quantities.

At The NoMad, our menus change with the seasons. Each menu features somewhere around 50 cocktails. We couldn't feature every recipe we've ever created in this book, so we chose more than 225 of our favorites and organized them the same way we do on our menu: Apéritifs, Light Spirited, Dark Spirited, Classics, and Soft Cocktails. Apéritifs are cocktails that are lower in alcohol content; their base is usually Champagne, beer, sherry, wine, or liqueurs. Light Spirited cocktails involve a base spirit that is not aged in oak (so vodka, gin, and the like), whereas Dark Spirited cocktails' base spirit is aged in oak (whiskey, Scotch, aged tequilas). The Classics chapter includes some less common, but historical recipes, as well as modern-day interpretations. Cocktail purists might argue that we take liberties with our "classics," and it's true that we do often modify the original source material. But any tweak we might make—such as changing a ratio or swapping or adding in more contemporary ingredients—is done to achieve what we believe is a more balanced drink. Soft Cocktails do not contain alcohol, but they are drinks in which we invest as much care and thought as we do in our cocktails to ensure all guests have something delicious to enjoy. The Basics chapter includes all the syrups and infusions you will need to create our recipes, as well as other building blocks for our cocktails.

You may notice that our recipes list ingredients in a different order than many other cocktail books do. We list in the order in which the ingredients should be added to the mixing vessel, and from smallest volume to largest (see Building Drinks, page 27, for our rationale). However, we also note the primary ingredients for each cocktail beneath each recipe title, with the most distinctive ingredients listed first, to help you better understand each cocktail at a glance.

Unless otherwise stated, we rely on the following rules:

All juice is fresh and double-strained

Butter is unsalted

Cream is heavy

Eggs are extra-large and organic

Herbs are fresh

Milk is whole

Salt is kosher

Sugar is granulated

And as I mentioned before, if at any point you have a question about a recipe or an ingredient, or want to talk cocktails or just say hello, please send us an email at cocktailbook@thenomadhotel.com. We are here to help.

SERVICE MANUAL

The bar at The NoMad is a bit different than most. We are in a restaurant in a hotel, open twenty-four hours a day, seven days a week, fifty-two weeks a year. And unlike many great cocktail bars around the country, every day we cater to guests who may not have walked into our building with the intention of enjoying a craft cocktail. It's for that reason that we choose to have a vast and diverse selection of drinks: some that may be classified as crowd-pleasers, others that are more adventurous, and some that may simply be called bartender drinks. But it's important to us that each individual drink be not only delicious and made to the highest standard, but that it also tell a story, whether that story is of seasonality, time and place, or sensory memory.

CREATING A COCKTAIL

When setting out to create new cocktails, many people jump in too quickly and try to mix together ingredients before they've developed an under-standing of the basics. You might be able to come up with a couple amazing cocktails with this approach, but it's not a sustainable method. First, you need to understand the intricacies of the ingredients—the flavors, and how they interact together—and this is only accomplished through research (and recipe testing). I recommend that new cocktail developers start by tasting through the classics, and using them as building blocks. Even today I find myself returning to the classics, as well as cocktails I developed earlier in my career, in order to improve upon them.

You may also think that adding additional ingredients to a drink is a good way to improve and balance a cocktail—but I'd argue it's better to streamline ingredients to achieve a more focused drink. For instance, do you need to use multiple amari in a drink, or will using one achieve the same result? You may be able to balance a twelve-ingredient cocktail, but can you really taste all of those components? Would a cocktail with four ingredients taste just as great?

Creating a cocktail requires an endgame; you should have a goal in mind before you even start measuring out your ingredients. For instance, an oatmeal cookie was the inspiration for the V.O.C. (page 109). I also love mulled cider, and that led to the creation of the Mott and Mulberry (page 145). Bottom line: Find your inspiration before you begin, whether it is an existing recipe such as a Sazerac, or a sensory memory you want to re-create.

Every cocktail has five base elements: the base spirit, sweetener, acid, bitter component, and dilution through water or ice. The easiest way to modify a cocktail is to change one of those ingredients at a time and test the result. (Note that some ingredients affect multiple base elements at a time, such as Champagne, apéritif liqueurs, herbal liqueurs, and sherries.) For example, our house recipe for a Manhattan calls for 2 dashes of Angostura bitters, 1 ounce of Carpano Antica Formula sweet vermouth, and 2 ounces of Rittenhouse bonded 100-proof rye whiskey, but many people ask for a Manhattan made with Old Overholt rye whiskey, which is 80 proof. Not only is the alcohol content different, but the flavors of the Old Overholt are more acidic and less woody than the Rittenhouse. So when creating a Manhattan with Old Overholt, we modify all the components to account for the differences, resulting in 4 dashes of bitters, 1 ounce of the same vermouth, but only 2½ ounces of the rye.

There are some instances when adding ingredients will improve upon a cocktail. I enjoy experimenting with multiple base spirits instead of one, a technique that is often used in tiki cocktails, and referred to as "split bases." Doing this allows you to achieve a flavor profile that may not exist in one product. I am especially fond of combining liquors that seem as if they would not play well together. For example, aquavit and Islay Scotch as seen in the North Sea Oil (page 146), rum and rye whiskey used in the Brown Sugar (page 118), or tequila and sherry, the base for the Paint it Black (page 94).

Sweeteners help balance acidity, bitterness, spice, and smokiness, and they can affect viscosity and mouthfeel. As you see in the Basics section, not all sweeteners have the same brix, which simply refers to the quantity of sugar in a liquid, nor do these sugars have the same flavor. If you take granulated, demerara, and muscovado sugars and make three simple syrups based on the same ratio, each one will have a different brix measurement, as well as varying characteristics. A basic daiquiri is made with 2 ounces of white rum, 1 ounce of lime juice, and ¾ ounce cane syrup (made in a 2:1 ratio with evaporated cane sugar). If we were to substitute a simple syrup made with granulated white sugar, we would change the recipe to follow a 2, ¾, and ¾ ratio of base spirit, citrus, and sweetener to achieve balance.

Not all citrus is the same, but the method for juicing it is. Be careful not to press down on the citrus too hard, as it will release bitterness within the pith and impact the flavor. Note that lemon and lime juice are not substitutes for one another, so when creating cocktails, I urge you to play with both and see how they differ. Oranges and grapefruits tend to be less acidic and have higher sugar content than lemons and limes, but again, they are not interchangeable.

There is an eighty-page service manual given to all new bartenders at The NoMad that goes into great detail about our methods, practices, and beliefs when it comes to making cocktails. I'm going to spare you all that extra reading and focus here on the areas that I believe make our cocktail program unique—the ingredients, tools, and techniques that distinguish our bar from others.

———

INGREDIENTS

In cocktails, just as in cooking, your dish or drink is only as good as your worst ingredient. In creating our recipes, we choose the spirit that works harmoniously with the other ingredients. This does not necessarily mean that the most expensive spirit is the right one. The price of a bottle of liquor is not always a guarantee of its quality, which is why I insist that every new staff member taste and analyze all the spirits we work with. Within each individual category of spirits, you need to take into account not only taste but also proof, because the proof of the spirit will affect the balance of the drink. You may be tempted to substitute your favorite spirit for the one listed in the recipe. If you do, take note of how the drink may have changed (its flavors and texture) and adjust accordingly to achieve the perfect balance. The same goes for all other ingredients listed.

GARNISHES

There are many different types of garnishes and even more methods of preparing them. We prefer to use fresh, organic, unwaxed fruits, vegetables, and herbs that are all washed and dried prior to preparing them as garnishes. All of our garnishes have a purpose, adding either flavors or aromas to complement the cocktail. Aesthetics are also important when thinking of garnishes, as your cocktails should always be photo-ready.

You may notice that our garnishes are more labor-intensive than others you come across. We prepare the majority of our garnishes before service to ensure quality and save time, due to the high volume of cocktails that we serve nightly.

Citrus Twist

Most bars use a vegetable peeler to cut their twists; at The NoMad we prefer a paring knife. This allows us to retain a small layer of pith, which extends the life of the twist, enabling us to prepare garnishes in advance of a busy service. To prepare a twist, first cut the ends of the fruit. Then start from the very top of one end and, following the shape of the fruit, cut all the way down to the other end. At this point, the twist should be about an inch wide. Clean up the twist by removing excess pith, leaving a minimal layer that is almost translucent (the more pith you leave on, the more unwanted bitterness your twist will bring to the cocktail). Cut the twist lengthwise and widthwise to clean up the edges. When expressing the oils from a twist, hold the twist between both index fingers and thumbs, about 6 inches above and 2 inches away from the drink to ensure that the oils evenly disperse over the cocktail. With the skin side of the twist facing toward the cocktail, squeeze, then wipe the twist around the edge of the glass and place it skin side up inside the cocktail when finished.

Flamed Twist

Flaming a twist caramelizes the citrus oils, which changes the aromas and flavors of the garnish before you express it over a cocktail. To garnish with a flamed twist, strike a match away from the cocktail so that the drink does not smell of sulfur. Use the lit match to warm both sides of a citrus peel. Then hold the match in one hand and the peel between the index finger and thumb of the other hand. Be sure to hold both about 6 inches from the cocktail, with the match between the peel and the glass. Quickly express the oils from the peel so that they ignite over the drink.

Horse's Neck

This is a twist that is cut around the entire piece of fruit. Follow the same steps, but start horizontally from the top and cut around the fruit in a corkscrew shape, being careful not to cut the twist until you reach the bottom of the fruit. This is a difficult garnish to prepare; it may take five or six attempts before you get it right, but it adds a lot visually to a drink.

Mint Plouche

A plouche is a collection of three or four mint tops, cleaned up and put together to resemble a flower (think carnation). We always smack the mint against our palms before placing it into the cocktail in order to release its aromatics.

Wheels and Half-Wheels

A wheel is a slice of citrus and a half-wheel is half a slice of citrus. Be sure to remove all seeds and cut your wheels the same exact width (approximately ¼ inch; we use a mandoline to prepare ours).

Cucumber Slice and Whole-Length Cucumber Slice

We use Japanese cucumbers, which have fewer seeds and tend to be uniform in width. Two types of cucumber garnishes are used at the bar: a disk-shaped slice, and a longer lengthwise slice that we use to wrap inside a drink (like a cucumber horse's neck). Both are sliced ⅛ inch thick, and we leave the cucumbers unpeeled.

Sugar and Salt Rims

To rim a glass with sugar or salt, moisten the top inch of the outer rim of a chilled glass, and gently roll the glass in sugar or salt. Use the corner of a folded cocktail napkin to make the sugar or salt a consistent thickness around the glass. Be sure to remove any sugar or salt from the inside of the glass.

Mound or Dome of Crushed Ice

This is less a garnish than part of the structure of certain drinks, such as juleps, that are brimming with crushed ice. To mound ice atop a cocktail, pack crushed ice into a julep strainer. Flip the strainer over the top of the glass and press the ice dome down to create a mounded ice dome up over the rim.

Floating

This is the process of adding a liquid ingredient on top of a cocktail with the purpose of slowly introducing a new flavor and adding visual appeal. The floating liquid will integrate as time passes, allowing for a cocktail to further develop. Be sure to pour the liquid slowly and as close to the top of the cocktail as possible.

———

TOOLS

In the recipes in this book, we list the specific tools we use to execute each drink at the restaurant. That being said, bartenders, much like chefs and carpenters, develop a specific relationship to their tools, and what may be the best spoon to me may be junk to another. You do not need an arsenal of fancy bar tools to execute a great cocktail—I've improvised in foreign situations and have used a straw as a spoon, or water bottle as a cocktail tin. However, if you want to accurately and consistently create the cocktails in this book, I encourage you to seek out all of the following tools. These are the items you shouldn't compromise on.

Jiggers

Every single bartender on staff uses them; they are the best way to maintain consistency and precision in measurement. We prefer Cocktail Kingdom's Japanese-style jiggers, which are slightly taller than other jiggers and, I find, more precise. When measuring ingredients, be sure to always hold your jigger to the side of the mixing glass (rather than over it) to prevent overflow from falling into the cocktail.

Barspoons

These are not the most accurate means of measurement, but can be useful for small amounts of liquid or dry ingredients. For consistency, use the same brand and style of spoon every time.

Dasher Bottles

Many cocktail recipes call for a "dash" of something, most often bitters. This is a vague form of measurement since each brand of bitters has a different top with a different-size aperture. The volume of the liquid in the bottle will also affect your measurements; bottles that are too full or those that are nearly empty may release less liquid. The best way to ensure consistency is to standardize your dasher bottles. We use Japanese dasher bottles from

ISI CANISTER

ATOMIZER

PARING KNIFE

TAPE

SHARPIE

MICROPLANE

REFRACTOMETER

DROPPER

TWEEZERS

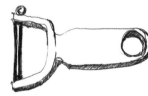

PEELER

MANDOLINE

Cocktail Kingdom with reusable metal screw caps. The Japanese dasher tops are significantly smaller than most bitters brands'; one dash from a normal bottle will be equivalent to three dashes in these bottles if you use a quick short dashing style, two if you use a longer dashing style. In this book, we'll consider "1 dash" to come from a Japanese bitters dasher.

Atomizers

We use atomizers—similar to a spray bottle used for perfume—to evenly distribute a small amount of a specific spirit or liqueur over the surface of a drink or to rinse a glass with a spirit or liqueur before the cocktail is strained into it. While this tool is not necessary, we find that it minimizes waste because it uses less product than pouring a small amount into a glass, and we recommend those available at specialtybottle.com.

iSi Canister with CO_2 (soda) and N_2O (cream) Chargers

The most common use for these canisters is to produce creams, foams, and carbonated drinks, but at the bar we've found this tool extremely useful for making rapid infusions. Of course, there are other ways to infuse a liquid with flavors and aromatics (and indeed, we don't think the iSi siphon method is ideal for every infusion); however, we believe it is the correct method for herbs and other bitter components that would typically become very tannic or take a long time to macerate. The process is this: When you charge an iSi canister with N_2O (nitrous oxide), the gas penetrates the solid particles of the flavoring agent. Later, when you vent the canister, the N_2O is dispersed through the liquid, infusing it with the flavoring agent. Practically speaking, you'll need an iSi cream canister and two N_2O chargers per infusion. Place the desired flavoring agent as well as the liquid to be infused into the canister. Seal the canister and charge it with two N_2O chargers, shaking it between each charge. Allow to sit for about 5 minutes. Then vent the canister by squeezing the handle until all the gas escapes. (Be sure to put a container underneath the nozzle while you're venting it in order to catch any liquid that comes out.) Open the canister and allow it to sit until the liquid stops bubbling—the bubbles indicate that the infusion is still in process. Strain the liquid and start making cocktails with the infusion.

Strainers

At The NoMad we use only hawthorne strainers; our preferred brand is Koriko from Cocktail Kingdom. Many people prefer to use a julep strainer for stirred drinks, but we find them too small for the Japanese-style mixing glasses that we use. We double-strain all of our shaken cocktails through a conical fine-mesh strainer, and prefer to use the Coco Strainer from Cocktail Kingdom.

In addition to jiggers, barspoons, dasher bottles, and iSi canister and chargers, you'll need basic bar supplies such as swizzles, mixing glasses, citrus juicers, peelers, knives, and cocktail tins for the recipes in this book. Each bartender has his or her favorites; I suggest you use those you are most comfortable with.

GLASSWARE

Each recipe in this book recommends a particular glass. I'm not suggesting you go out and purchase dozens of different glasses in various shapes and sizes, but it's true that the glass in which your cocktail is served will impact its aroma and flavor. We stock the following glasses at The NoMad: Nick and Nora (6 ounces), tulip (6 ounces), fortified (7 ounces), hot-cocktail (8 ounces), fizz (9 ounces), single rocks (9½ ounces), coupe (9¾ ounces), cobbler (11½ ounces), highball (12 ounces), Pilsner (12 ounces), double rocks (14 ounces), Belgian (15 ounces), rooster cup or tiki mug (18 ounces), snifter (19 ounces), and explosion vessel (192 ounces).

ICE

It's important to understand that not all ice is created equal. What may work for one drink could vastly dilute another. There are entire essays devoted to the topic of ice in cocktails, but I'll only dive into what I believe to be true and essential. Ice in cocktails serves two basic purposes: to chill a drink, and to dilute a drink. The amount of dilution, or the degree to which you chill a drink, depends on the size and type of ice you use. At The NoMad we use three different sizes of ice: Kold Draft (a clear, solid 1¼-inch cube made in a Kold Draft brand machine); Scotsman pellet ice (crushed ice made in a Scotsman brand machine); and 2-inch cubes, which are either made in molds or purchased from a specialty ice store.

There are also two different types of ice: wet and dry. For our purposes, "dry ice" does *not* refer to solid carbon dioxide—rather, we use "dry" to describe ice that is sticky to the touch, as it would be if you had just pulled it from the freezer. Wet ice, by contrast, is moist when you touch it, due to the water that adheres to the surface. Both types of ice are okay, but I prefer to use drier ice for shaking, as it allows us to shake the cocktail for a longer period of time, incorporating more air, and achieving a frothier head. You can use either ice for stirring, but wet ice will speed the process, allowing you to more quickly achieve the sought-after result.

At home, of course, I don't expect you to have access to a Kold Draft or Scotsman ice machine. But each type of ice does serve a different purpose, so I encourage you to seek out ice molds that mirror the different shapes and sizes we use. Use purified water, as it will affect the flavor of your drink. Also, know that ice will absorb the odors around it, so make sure that your freezer is odor-free when you're making your ice—you wouldn't want last night's chicken parm leftovers flavoring your daiquiri. In the recipes, you'll note that I call for shaking and stirring cocktails over 1¼-inch cubes, which might be difficult if you're relying on ice molds. Realistically, you can use any type of ice for shaking and stirring drinks—reserve the good stuff for serving—but be mindful of the fact that variable sizes of ice will affect the dilution of your cocktail.

1¼-inch Ice Cubes

Ours come from a Kold Draft machine; however, you can buy 1¼-inch silicone molds online and in stores. I recommend Tovolo brand. We use 1¼-inch cubes for shaking cocktails, and for serving in highball or small rocks glasses.

2-Inch Ice Cubes

Again, I recommend Tovolo brand silicone molds for these. Use this type of ice for shaking egg white or cream drinks, as it helps produce a more frothy head. It is also recommended for serving tequila, rum, whiskey, and amaro on the rocks, or in stirred cocktails served in anything larger than a single rocks glass.

Crushed Ice

At home you can simply use an ice crusher, Lewis bag (or other clean canvas sack) and mallet, or my favorite, a Snoopy sno-cone maker. If you're crushing your ice by hand, be sure to dry it off afterward with a paper towel or spin it in a salad spinner. This will ensure you do not add extra, unwanted dilution to your beverages. Use this type of ice for juleps, crustas, mojitos, caipirinhas, smashes, mai tais, or zombies.

TECHNIQUES

There are many different ways to make a cocktail, and each technique serves a specific purpose. Shaking is different than stirring, and there is a reason why we muddle some drinks but not others. Here are some important guidelines to help you in creating just about any cocktail.

Shaking and Stirring

One of the most basic questions I'm often asked is the difference between shaking and stirring a drink. Both methods accomplish three things: mixing of the ingredients, dilution through ice, and chilling of the drink. The main difference is that shaking aerates the cocktail, creating a more frothy texture and changing its appearance. Aeration also adds perceived dilution because the ingredients are less concentrated. Stirring, by contrast, accomplishes mixing, dilution, and chilling, but not aeration.

SHAKING GUIDELINES

- Most cocktails that have juice, egg, milk, or cream are shaken—often dry shaken, or shaken without ice. These ingredients have significantly different densities than most spirits, so cocktails that include them require more energy in order to be made homogeneous—think of combining oil and water. If you stir the ingredients, they stay separated, but if you shake it vigorously, they become one.

- For shaking cocktails, we use a Boston or two-piece tin. Build all shaken cocktails in the smaller tin. Fill it with ice and then place the larger tin over the top. Shake with the smaller tin facing you and the larger tin facing away from you to make sure that any liquid that escapes from the seal does not hit your guests.

- To break the seal on the tins, push the smaller tin away from the initial point of separation. Never hit the tins against any surface as it may damage them.

STIRRING GUIDELINES

- Assess your ice before stirring. If the ice is dry and new, you may want to crack a few cubes to increase the surface area of the ice; this will allow you to reach your desired dilution and temperature more quickly. If the ice is wet, no cracking is needed.

- The term "wash line" is the point where the ice meets the liquid in the mixing glass. In most cases, the wash line for a perfectly diluted cocktail should fall just below the top of the ice. Stirring drinks that are going on the rocks should be underdiluted (the wash line should be lower).

- Always taste your drinks while stirring. It's the only way to gauge proper dilution and to guarantee you've made the drink correctly. Be sure to use a brand-new straw or clean barspoon every time you taste in order not to contaminate the beverage.

Swizzling and Whipping

Swizzling involves using a specific tool (a swizzle stick or *bois lélé* branch) to stir a drink that is served over crushed ice in its serving glass. In fact, swizzling is most like shaking in that mixing, chilling, dilution, and aeration are accomplished. The majority of the dilution happens quickly due to the water adhered to the crushed ice, which has a larger combined surface area than cube ice.

One main purpose of swizzling is to convert the serving glass into an extremely cold insulator—frequent contact with the crushed ice helps the glass quickly reach and maintain a very cold temperature.

Whipping is the process of shaking with minimal ice (we use three 1¼-inch cubes), aerating a drink while providing limited dilution. This is done with drinks served over crushed ice and mimics the process that occurs in swizzling. At The NoMad we choose to whip the majority of our drinks that we might otherwise swizzle, since swizzling takes more time, but you can use either method at home.

Muddling

At The NoMad, we do not actually "muddle" any herbs—we gently tamp them in whichever sweetener is used in a recipe. Muddling herbs—pressing with a pestle or muddler—extracts tannins and other bitter, muddy flavors that are unwanted in most cocktails. For the purposes of this book we use "muddle" as shorthand—but in those instances you should only gently press the herbs with your muddler.

There is no need to muddle the herbs in any cocktails that are shaken. The ice will work as a muddler and extract all your essential oils and desired aromas.

Straining

In the case of shaken cocktails, we always double-strain them. We place a hawthorne strainer atop a conical fine-mesh strainer, then strain the drink through both directly into the glass. While this is not common practice at most other bars, we find that it improves the quality of a cocktail, removing any small pieces of ice or other unwanted particles that may affect the texture.

————

BUILDING DRINKS

At home you will probably be creating one cocktail at a time, investing all of your focus and energy on that one specific drink. At The NoMad, our staff is shaking, stirring, and whipping numerous drinks at the same time in order to serve the hundreds of guests we welcome on a nightly basis. The following steps reflect how we build a round of drinks in order to maximize efficiency, provide a high level of service, and maintain quality control while getting the drinks out as fast as we can.

Before You Make Your Drink

· Always start with the smallest-volume ingredient and build your drink up from there. In most instances the order will be something like bitters, sugar, citrus, and so on. The logic here is that if you start with the smaller measurements, you leave yourself more room for error. If you make a mistake, it's far less painful to throw out a dash of bitters than a couple of ounces of a spirit.

· Never fill your tin or mixing glass with ice until you are ready to stir. You may be distracted before finishing your cocktail, and the ice can dilute your drink more than desired.

· Don't rinse out your jigger immediately after using honey, cane syrup, or other viscous sweeteners; reuse that jigger as you build your drink to ensure you get the full amount of sweetener into the glass.

· When creating a drink with eggs, always crack the egg on a hard surface and then add it to the larger of your tins, to ensure that you don't get shell in the drink. We use an egg separator, as the outside of the egg shell can be dirty or harbor impurities.

· Glassware should (almost) always be chilled. Any exceptions will be called out in the recipe.

Step-by-Step

Here are our steps of service when building a round of drinks:

1. Pull and prepare your garnishes.

2. Build each drink in the appropriate cocktail tin or mixing vessel. If you are building two, but no more than two, you can combine them into one tin or mixing vessel, making sure to add more ice, and stir or shake longer to achieve the desired dilution. If using a two-piece shaker, build the drink in the smaller tin.

3. Retrieve your chilled glassware.

4. Dry shake (shake without ice) all cream- or egg-based cocktails.

5. Add ice and any primers (such as rinses) to your serving glassware.

6. Prepare each cocktail in order of mixing method: first swizzle, then whip, then stir, then shake. For shaken drinks, you should always strain into the serving glass immediately after shaking. Other drinks can be strained or double-strained after the entire round is built.

7. If the drink calls for bitters as a finishing agent, add it now.

8. Top with any other finishing liquids, such as beer, wine, or soda, if needed.

9. Garnish, and serve with a good attitude.

10. Clean your tools and repeat—many, many times.

11. Go for numerous shift drinks after service; I usually prefer whiskey.

ELEVEN NON-NEGOTIABLES
FOR A NOMAD BARTENDER

1. Greet every guest with a warm smile and a menu upon arrival.

2. Maintain a clean and composed appearance, as a bar and as an individual.

3. Take pride in our craft by properly measuring, mixing, and garnishing every cocktail.

4. Understand our food and beverage knowledge as true professionals.

5. Acknowledge and serve every guest, even when not in your station.

6. Label checks and assure we are accurate with all of our transactions.

7. Remember we are on stage and are here to create a welcoming environment and to entertain.

8. Respect all our spaces, colleagues, and tools.

9. Build rounds of drinks to ensure quality, speed, and accuracy.

10. When we can, we are cleaning, labeling, marrying, and organizing the back bar.

11. Push to be better than we were yesterday.

APÉRITIFS

8TH WONDER

A bitter highball with hints of grapefruit

———

Caperetif, Barolo Chinato, Elderflower Liqueur, Grapefruit, Lime

- ½ ounce lime juice
- ¾ ounce St-Germain
- ¾ ounce Cocchi Barolo Chinato
- 1½ ounces Caperetif
- 1 ounce Fever-Tree tonic water

In a cocktail tin, combine all the ingredients except the tonic water. Fill a highball glass with 1¼-inch ice cubes. Prime the highball glass with the tonic water. Cover the cocktail tin and shake. Strain the cocktail into the highball glass.

GLASS: Highball   ICE: 1¼-inch cubes   CREATOR: Pietro Collina

ANGELO AND ROCCO

A bitter sour with flavors of black pepper and apples

———

Punt e Mes, Amaro Abano, Amontillado Sherry, Apple Cider, Lemon, Black Pepper

- ½ ounce Tellicherry Black Pepper Syrup (page 248)
- ½ ounce lemon juice
- ¾ ounce Lustau Los Arcos amontillado sherry
- ¾ ounce Honeycrisp apple cider
- ¾ ounce Luxardo Amaro Abano
- 1 ounce Carpano Punt e Mes vermouth

Combine all the ingredients in a cocktail tin. Fill the tin with ice, cover, and shake vigorously. Strain the cocktail into a coupe.

GLASS: Coupe   ICE: None   CREATOR: Leo Robitschek

ANTHORA

Amaro cobbler with coffee and fennel

Averna, Punt e Mes, Aquavit, Coffee, Lemon

½ ounce Cane Syrup (page 218)

½ ounce Krogstad aquavit

¾ ounce Cold Brew Coffee Concentrate (page 226)

¾ ounce lemon juice

¾ ounce Carpano Punt e Mes vermouth

1 ounce Averna

Mint plouche, for garnish

Grapefruit twist, for garnish

In a cocktail tin, combine all the ingredients except the garnishes. Fill a cobbler glass with crushed ice. Add three 1¼-inch ice cubes to the cocktail tin. Cover and whip. Strain the cocktail into the cobbler glass and top with additional crushed ice. Garnish with the mint plouche and grapefruit twist.

GLASS: Cobbler   ICE: Crushed   CREATOR: Leo Robitschek

BANANA STAND

A sherry cobbler with flavors of banana and chocolate

Banana-Infused Oloroso Sherry, Venezuelan Rum, Falernum, Pineapple Gomme, Brown Butter, Chocolate, Salt

4 dashes Bitter Truth chocolate bitters
10 drops Saline Solution (page 245)
½ ounce Pineapple Gomme (page 240)
½ ounce Brown Butter Falernum (page 218)
½ ounce Diplomático Reserva Exclusiva rum
2 ounces Banana Oloroso (page 216)
72 percent bittersweet chocolate, for garnish

In a cocktail tin, combine all the ingredients except the garnish. Fill a Pilsner glass with crushed ice. Add three 1¼-inch ice cubes to the cocktail tin. Cover and whip. Strain the cocktail into the Pilsner glass and top with additional crushed ice. Shave bittersweet chocolate over the top of the cocktail for garnish.

GLASS: Pilsner   ICE: Crushed   CREATOR: Leo Robitschek

BROKEN SPANISH

A lower–ABV martini with vinous and herbaceous flavors

Fino Sherry, Cocchi Americano, Bénédictine, Verjus

½ ounce Bénédictine
1 ounce Fusion verjus blanc juice
1 ounce Cocchi Americano
1½ ounces Lustau Jarana fino sherry
Becherovka, as a rinse
Grapefruit twist, for garnish

In a chilled mixing glass, combine all the ingredients except the Becherovka and garnish. Fill the mixing glass with 1¼-inch ice cubes and stir. Using an atomizer, rinse a chilled coupe with six sprays of Becherovka. Strain the cocktail into the coupe. Express the grapefruit twist over the drink and then drop it into the glass.

GLASS: Coupe   ICE: None   CREATOR: Pietro Collina

BULLINGDON CLUB CUP

A bitter and vegetal watermelon cooler

———

Aperol, Rabarbaro, Watermelon, Celery, Black Pepper, Lemon, Basil, Salt

Lemon wedge, for rimming
Salt, for rimming
5 basil leaves
½ ounce Tellicherry Black Pepper Syrup (page 248)
½ ounce celery juice
¾ ounce lemon juice
¾ ounce Donna Rosa Rabarbaro
¾ ounce Aperol
1 ounce watermelon juice
1 ounce cold Fever-Tree tonic water, plus more to finish

Use the lemon wedge to moisten the top inch of the outer rim of a chilled highball glass. Gently roll the highball glass in salt to rim half of the glass. Shake off excess salt. Use the corner of a folded cocktail napkin to make the salt a consistent thickness. Fill the highball glass with 1¼-inch ice cubes. Add all the remaining ingredients except the tonic water to a cocktail tin. Add three 1¼-inch ice cubes to the tin. Cover and whip vigorously. Add the tonic water to the tin. Strain the cocktail into the highball glass using a hawthorne strainer. Fill the glass with additional tonic water.

GLASS: Highball   ICE: 1¼-inch cubes   CREATOR: Pietro Collina

CARDINALE

A refreshing cobbler with notes of grapefruit and ginger

Barolo Chinato, Fino Sherry, Rabarbaro Zucca Amaro, Lemon, Grapefruit, Ginger, Cucumber

2 cucumber slices, 1 for muddling and 1 for garnish
¼ ounce Spicy Ginger Syrup (page 247)
½ ounce Rabarbaro Zucca amaro
½ ounce Lustau Jarana fino sherry
¾ ounce grapefruit juice
¾ ounce lemon juice
1½ ounces Cocchi Barolo Chinato
½ ounce Seagram's club soda

In a cocktail tin, muddle a cucumber slice in the ginger syrup, then add the remaining ingredients except the club soda and garnish. Fill a highball glass with crushed ice. Add three 1¼-inch cubes to the tin. Cover and whip. Strain the cocktail into the highball glass. Add the club soda and garnish with the remaining cucumber slice.

GLASS: Highball   ICE: Crushed   CREATOR: Gino Pellarin

CLIP JOINT CUP

A bitter Pimm's Cup variation

Punt e Mes, Amaro Averna, Lime, Ginger,
Grapefruit, Cucumber, Tonic

2 grapefruit twists, 1 for muddling and
1 for garnish

2 cucumber slices, 1 for muddling and
1 for garnish

½ ounce Demerara Simple Syrup (page 227)

¾ ounce Seagram's club soda

¾ ounce Fever-Tree tonic water

½ ounce Ginger Lime Syrup (page 231)

¾ ounce lime juice

1 ounce Amaro Averna

1 ounce Carpano Punt e Mes vermouth

Mint plouche, for garnish

In a cocktail tin, muddle a grapefruit twist and a cucumber slice with
the demerara syrup. Fill a highball glass with 1¼-inch ice cubes and
prime it with the club soda and tonic water. Add the rest of the ingredients
except the garnishes to the tin. Cover and shake. Strain the cocktail into
the highball glass. Garnish with the mint plouche and remaining cucumber
slice and grapefruit twist.

GLASS: Highball   ICE: 1¼-inch cubes   CREATOR: Leo Robitschek

COMMON THREAD

A lightly savory and refreshing cooler

Cocchi Americano, Chareau, Suze, Fino Sherry, Grapefruit, Lemon, Jalapeño-Infused Agave, Absinthe

Lemon wedge, for rimming
Aleppo chile salt, for rimming
4 dashes Pernod Absinthe
½ ounce Jalapeño-Infused Agave Syrup (page 235)
½ ounce lemon juice
½ ounce grapefruit juice
½ ounce Chareau liqueur
½ ounce Suze
¾ ounce Lustau Jarana fino sherry
1 ounce Cocchi Americano
1½ ounces Seagram's club soda
Whole-length cucumber slice, for garnish

Use the lemon wedge to moisten the top inch of the outer rim of a chilled highball glass. Gently roll the highball glass in chile salt to rim half of the glass. Shake off excess salt. Use the corner of a folded cocktail napkin to make the salt a consistent thickness. Fill the highball glass with 1¼-inch ice cubes. Add the remaining ingredients except the club soda and garnish to a cocktail tin. Add three 1¼-inch ice cubes to the tin. Cover and shake vigorously. Add 1 ounce of the club soda to the cocktail tin. Strain the cocktail into the highball glass using a hawthorne strainer. Fill the glass with the remaining ½ ounce club soda and garnish with the cucumber slice around the inside rim of the glass.

GLASS: Highball   ICE: 1¼-inch cubes   CREATOR: Julia Reingold

CORTEZ

A savory Champagne cocktail

Champagne, Amontillado Sherry, Lemon, Ceylon Cinnamon

> ¼ ounce Simple Syrup (page 245)
> ¾ ounce Ceylon Cinnamon Syrup (page 219)
> ¾ ounce lemon juice
> 1½ ounces Lustau Los Arcos amontillado sherry
> 2 ounces Duc de Romet Champagne

Combine all the ingredients except the Champagne in a cocktail tin. Fill a highball glass with 1¼-inch ice cubes and add the Champagne. Fill the cocktail tin with ice. Cover and shake vigorously. Strain the cocktail into the highball glass.

GLASS: Highball   ICE: 1¼-inch cubes   CREATOR: Ryan Curran

CUP OF JOE

A Pimm's Cup variation with coffee, grapefruit, and vanilla

Coffee-Infused Vermouth, Amaro Abano, Grapefruit, Lemon, Cinnamon, Vanilla

> ¼ ounce Vanilla Syrup (page 249)
> ¼ ounce Ceylon Cinnamon Syrup (page 219)
> ½ ounce lemon juice
> ¾ ounce grapefruit juice
> 1 ounce Luxardo Amaro Abano
> 1 ounce Coffee-Infused Dry Vermouth (page 226)
> 1 ounce Fever-Tree tonic water
> Grapefruit twist, for expressing

In a cocktail tin, combine all the ingredients except the tonic water and grapefruit twist. Fill a highball glass with 1¼-inch ice cubes. Prime the highball glass with the tonic water. Cover the cocktail tin and shake. Strain the cocktail into the highball glass. Express the oils of the grapefruit twist over the drink, then discard the twist.

GLASS: Highball   ICE: 1¼-inch cubes   CREATOR: Shaun Dunn

DANGER HAUS

A bitter, cranberry-forward sherry cobbler

Fino Sherry, Suze, Grapefruit Oleo Saccharum, Cranberry, Cucumber

   1 teaspoon Grapefruit Oleo Saccharum (page 231)
   ½ ounce lemon juice
   1 ounce Cranberry Syrup (page 227)
   1 ounce Suze
   1½ ounces Lustau Jarana fino sherry
   Whole-length cucumber slice, for garnish

Combine all the ingredients except the garnish in a cocktail tin. Wrap
the cucumber slice around the inside of the highball glass, starting
from the bottom, and fill the glass with crushed ice. Add three 1½-inch
ice cubes to the cocktail tin. Cover and whip. Strain the cocktail into
the highball glass.

GLASS: Highball   ICE: Crushed   CREATORS: Jane Danger
                                               and Pietro Collina

FOLKLORE

A fall-flavored shandy with cinnamon and pear

Saison Ale, Amontillado Sherry, Spiced Pear Liqueur, Lemon,
Ceylon Cinnamon

   1 teaspoon Cane Syrup (page 218)
   ½ ounce St. George spiced pear liqueur
   ½ ounce Ceylon Cinnamon Syrup (page 219)
   ½ ounce lemon juice
   1 ounce Lustau Los Arcos amontillado sherry
   3 ounces Folksbier Sif dry-hopped table beer

In a cocktail tin, combine all the ingredients except the beer. Fill a highball
glass with 1¼-inch ice cubes and add the beer. Fill the tin with ice. Cover
and shake vigorously. Strain the cocktail into the highball glass.

GLASS: Highball   ICE: 1¼-inch cubes   CREATORS: Pietro Collina
                                                     and Julia Reingold

FRESA Y CERVESA

A tart and vegetal shandy with flavors of strawberry

———

Berliner Weiss, Yellow Chartreuse, Strawberry Shrub, Jalapeño, Agave, Lemon

Cucumber slice, for muddling, plus
whole-length cucumber slice, for garnish

½ ounce yellow Chartreuse

½ ounce lemon juice

¾ ounce Strawberry Pickling Liquid (page 247)

¾ ounce Jalapeño-Infused Agave Syrup (page 235)

2 ounces Evil Twin Nomader Weisse

In a cocktail tin, muddle a cucumber slice and combine the remaining ingredients except the beer and garnish. Wrap the cucumber garnish around the inside of a highball glass, starting from the bottom. Fill the glass with 1¼-inch ice cubes and add the beer. Add ice to the tin. Cover and shake vigorously. Strain the cocktail into the highball glass.

GLASS: Highball   ICE: 1¼-inch cubes   CREATOR: Leo Robitschek

HAYMARKET

A bitter and refreshing shandy

———

Pale Ale, Suze, Lemon, Cucumber

2 cucumber slices, 1 for muddling and 1 for garnish, plus whole-length cucumber slice, for garnish

¾ ounce Simple Syrup (page 245)

¾ ounce lemon juice

1 ounce Suze

2 ounces Two Brothers pale ale

In a cocktail tin, muddle a cucumber slice and combine the remaining ingredients except the beer and the garnish. Wrap the whole-length cucumber garnish around the inside of a highball glass, starting from the bottom. Fill the glass with 1¼-inch ice cubes and add the beer. Fill the tin with ice. Cover and shake vigorously. Strain the cocktail into the highball glass and garnish with the remaining cucumber slice.

GLASS: Highball   ICE: 1¼-inch cubes   CREATOR: Leo Robitschek

HOT BROTH

A savory boozy brodo with an anise undertone

Amontillado Sherry, Absinthe, Spiced Tomato Water, Chicken Jus

6 dashes Pernod Absinthe
1 teaspoon Chicken Jus (page 222)
1½ ounces Lustau Los Arcos amontillado sherry
5 ounces Spiced Tomato Water (page 246)

Fill a hot-cocktail glass with hot water in order to heat it. In a small saucepan, combine all the ingredients and warm over medium heat until the cocktail comes to a simmer. Discard the hot water in the cocktail glass, then pour in the cocktail.

GLASS: Hot-cocktail   ICE: None   CREATOR: Shaun Dunn

HOWIE IN THE JUNGLE

A bitter sling with cherry and pineapple

Zucca, Aperol, Cherry Heering, Pineapple, Lime

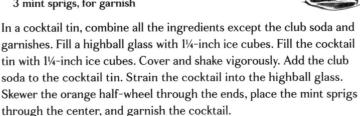

1 teaspoon Passionfruit Syrup (page 240)
½ ounce Cherry Heering
Scant ¾ ounce lime juice
¾ ounce pineapple juice
¾ ounce Aperol
1½ ounces Rabarbaro Zucca amaro
1 ounce Seagram's club soda
Orange half-wheel, for garnish
3 mint sprigs, for garnish

In a cocktail tin, combine all the ingredients except the club soda and garnishes. Fill a highball glass with 1¼-inch ice cubes. Fill the cocktail tin with 1¼-inch ice cubes. Cover and shake vigorously. Add the club soda to the cocktail tin. Strain the cocktail into the highball glass. Skewer the orange half-wheel through the ends, place the mint sprigs through the center, and garnish the cocktail.

GLASS: Highball   ICE: 1¼-inch cubes   CREATOR: Nathan O'Neill

INTO THE WOODS

A light sour with maple and pine

Chambery Blanc Vermouth, Douglas Fir Liqueur, Maple Syrup, Lemon, Egg White

1 egg white
½ ounce Grade A maple syrup
¾ ounce lemon juice
1 ounce Brovo Douglas Fir liqueur
1½ ounces Dolin de Chambery Blanc vermouth
Rosemary sprig, for garnish

In a cocktail tin, combine all the ingredients except the garnish. Seal the tin and dry shake to emulsify the egg white into the cocktail. Carefully open the tin and fill with 1¼-inch ice cubes. Seal it again and shake vigorously. Strain the cocktail into a chilled coupe using a hawthorne strainer and a fine tea strainer. Garnish with the sprig of rosemary.

GLASS: Coupe   ICE: None   CREATOR: Leo Robitschek

JANE STANLEY

A bitter sour with orange

Amontillado Sherry, Amaro Ciociaro, Orange, Lemon

3 orange half-wheels, 1 for muddling and 2 for garnish
Scant ½ ounce Cane Syrup (page 218)
¾ ounce lemon juice
1 ounce Amaro Ciociaro
1½ ounces Lustau Los Arcos amontillado sherry

In a cocktail tin, muddle an orange half-wheel, then add the remaining ingredients except the garnish. Fill a cobbler glass with crushed ice. Add three 1¼-inch ice cubes to the cocktail tin. Cover and whip. Strain the cocktail into the cobbler glass and garnish with the remaining orange half-wheels.

GLASS: Cobbler   ICE: Crushed   CREATOR: Leo Robitschek

JOE DANGER

A vermouth sour with coffee and grapefruit

Sweet Vermouth, Coffee-Infused Dry Vermouth,
Pale Cream Sherry, Lemon, Angostura Bitters

4 dashes Angostura bitters
½ ounce Simple Syrup (page 245)
½ ounce lemon juice
¾ ounce Coffee-Infused Dry Vermouth (page 226)
¾ ounce Alvear Pale cream sherry
¾ ounce Carpano Antica Formula sweet vermouth
¾ ounce Lustau Vermut Rojo vermouth
Grapefruit twist, for garnish
Mint plouche, for garnish

Combine all the ingredients except the garnishes in a cocktail tin. Fill a
Pilsner glass with crushed ice. Add three 1¼-inch ice cubes to the cocktail
tin. Cover and whip. Strain the cocktail into the Pilsner glass and top
with additional crushed ice. Express the oils of the grapefruit twist over
the top of the drink. Garnish with the mint plouche and the expressed
grapefruit twist.

GLASS: Pilsner   ICE: Crushed   CREATOR: Jane Danger

MA CHERIE

A lightly savory and refreshing cooler

Fino Sherry, Green Chartreuse, Velvet Falernum, Lime, Cucumber, Celery, Salt, Pineapple Gomme

1-inch piece celery, for muddling
10 drops Saline Solution (page 245)
¼ ounce green Chartreuse
¼ ounce John D. Taylor's Velvet Falernum
½ ounce Pineapple Gomme (page 240)
½ ounce lime juice
2½ ounces Lustau Jarana fino sherry
Whole-length cucumber slice, for garnish

In a cocktail tin, muddle the celery, then combine all the remaining ingredients except the garnish. Wrap the cucumber garnish around the inside of a highball glass, starting from the bottom. Fill the highball glass with crushed ice. Add three 1¼-inch ice cubes to the cocktail tin. Cover and whip. Strain the cocktail into the highball glass.

GLASS: Highball   ICE: Crushed   CREATOR: Leo Robitschek

MIDNIGHT BRAMBLE

A refreshing sour with blackberries

Fino Sherry, Bonal, Crème de Mûre, Lemon, Blackberries

Scant ½ ounce Simple Syrup (page 245)
¾ ounce lemon juice
¾ ounce Bonal
1 ounce Lustau Jarana fino sherry
5 medium blackberries, for garnish
½ ounce Massenez Crème de Mûre, to finish

Combine all the ingredients except the blackberries and crème de mûre in a cocktail tin. Place the blackberries on the bottom of a double rocks glass and fill the glass with crushed ice. Add three 1¼-inch cubes to the cocktail tin. Cover and whip. Strain the cocktail into the double rocks glass. Fill the glass with more crushed ice and make a mound of crushed ice up over the rim of the glass. Pour the crème de mûre over the top of the dome.

GLASS: Double rocks   ICE: Crushed   CREATOR: Leo Robitschek

MONFERRATO

A Champagne cocktail with bitter orange notes

Champagne, Cocchi Americano, Triple Sec,
Peychaud's Bitters, Angostura Bitters

    6 dashes Angostura bitters
    6 dashes Peychaud's bitters
    ½ ounce Combier triple sec
    1 ounce Cocchi Americano
    2 ounces Duc de Romet Champagne
    Orange twist, for expressing

Combine all the ingredients except the Champagne and orange twist in
a mixing glass. Fill the mixing glass with ice and stir. Strain the cocktail
into a Champagne flute and top with Champagne. Express the oils of
the orange twist over the glass, then rub the twist on the rim of the glass
and discard the twist.

GLASS: Champagne flute   ICE: None   CREATOR: Leo Robitschek

ON THE VINE

A savory and tart sour full of tomato flavor

Fino Sherry, Amontillado Sherry, Tomato Water, Lemon, White Balsamic Vinegar, Salt

15 drops Saline Solution (page 245)
Scant ½ ounce Cane Syrup (page 218)
½ ounce Lustau Los Arcos amontillado sherry
1 ounce Spiced Tomato Water (page 246)
2 ounces Lustau Jarana fino sherry
3 dashes white balsamic vinegar
½ ounce lemon juice
Lemon thyme sprig, for garnish

Using an iSi canister (see page 22), carbonate the saline solution, cane syrup, amontillado sherry, tomato water, and fino sherry. Place a 2-inch ice cube in a double rocks glass. Add the vinegar, lemon juice, and 4 ounces of the carbonated liquid to the rocks glass and stir gently for 5 seconds. Garnish with the sprig of lemon thyme.

GLASS: Double rocks   ICE: 2-inch cube   CREATOR: Leo Robitschek

SEOUL MATE

A sherry cobbler with peach and almond

Amontillado Sherry, Vermouth di Torino, Crème de Pêche, Orgeat, Lemon

½ ounce Massenez Crème de Pêche
½ ounce Orgeat (page 239)
½ ounce lemon juice
¾ ounce Cocchi Vermouth di Torino
2 ounces Lustau Los Arcos amontillado sherry
Lemon wheel, for garnish

In a cocktail tin, combine all the ingredients except the garnish. Fill a highball glass with crushed ice. Add three 1¼-inch ice cubes to the cocktail tin. Cover and whip. Strain the cocktail into the highball glass and top with additional crushed ice. Garnish with the lemon wheel.

GLASS: Highball   ICE: Crushed   CREATORS: Leo Robitschek
                                                and Pietro Collina

SHIITAKE DIRTY TO ME

A smoky and umami-forward Old-Fashioned

Amontillado Sherry, Mushroom Broth, Squash, Honey,
Verjus, Coffee, Angostura Bitters

8 dashes Coffee-Infused Angostura Bitters (page 225)
1 teaspoon Fusion verjus blanc juice
¼ ounce Honey Syrup (page 233)
Scant ½ ounce Kabocha Squash Syrup (page 236)
1 ounce Mushroom Broth (page 238)
1½ ounces Lustau Los Arcos amontillado sherry
Laphroaig 10-Year Scotch, to finish

In a double rocks glass, combine all the ingredients except the Scotch.
Add a 2-inch ice cube and stir for 5 seconds. Using an atomizer, top
the double rocks glass with six sprays of Scotch.

GLASS: Double rocks   ICE: 2-inch cube   CREATOR: Shaun Dunn

SHUTTLECOCK

A sangria variation with bitter cherry and mint

Cabernet Franc, Moscatel Sherry,
Maraschino Liqueur, Yellow Chartreuse,
Lemon, Blackberries, Mint, Orange

5 mint leaves, for muddling

4 blackberries, 3 for muddling and
1 for garnish

Orange half-wheel, for muddling,
plus orange wheel, for garnish

½ ounce Luxardo Maraschino liqueur

½ ounce Luxardo Amaro Abano

½ ounce yellow Chartreuse

¾ ounce Lustau Emelín Moscatel sherry

¾ ounce lemon juice

1½ ounces Cabernet Franc

½ ounce Seagram's club soda, to finish

Mint plouche, for garnish

In a cocktail tin, muddle the mint leaves, three of the blackberries, and
the orange half-wheel, then add the remaining ingredients except the
club soda and garnishes. Fill a Pilsner glass with crushed ice. Add three
1¼-inch ice cubes to the cocktail tin. Cover and whip. Strain the cocktail
into the Pilsner glass and add the club soda. Skewer the remaining orange
wheel and blackberry to create a flag, then garnish with the mint plouche
and the orange-blackberry flag.

GLASS: Pilsner   ICE: Crushed   CREATOR: Pietro Collina

SIPPY CUP

A bitter cup with ginger and lime

Amaro Averna, Vermouth de Torino,
Ginger, Lime

¾ ounce Spicy Ginger Syrup (page 247)

1 ounce lime juice

1 ounce Cocchi Vermouth di Torino

1½ ounces Amaro Averna

2 dashes Angostura bitters, to finish

1 ounce Seagram's club soda, to finish

Orange half-wheel, for garnish

3 mint sprigs, for garnish

In a cocktail tin, combine the ginger syrup, lime juice, vermouth, and amaro. Fill a highball glass with 1¼-inch ice cubes. Fill the cocktail tin with ice. Cover and shake vigorously. Strain the cocktail into the highball glass. Add the Angostura bitters to the top of the cocktail and top with the club soda. Skewer the orange half-wheel through the ends and place the mint sprigs through the center, then garnish the cocktail with the orange-mint flag.

GLASS: Highball   ICE: 1¼-inch cubes   CREATOR: Leo Robitschek

SUMMER OF YES

A shandy with elderflower and jalapeño

Berliner Weisse, Elderflower Liqueur, Rhubarb Shrub, Agave, Lemon, Jalapeño, Cucumber, Salt

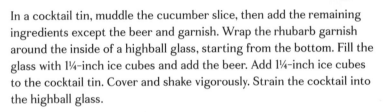

Cucumber slice, for muddling
½ ounce Jalapeño-Infused Agave Syrup (page 235)
½ ounce lemon juice
½ ounce Rhubarb Shrub (page 243)
1 ounce St-Germain
3 ounces Evil Twin Nomader Weisse
Whole-length rhubarb slice, for garnish

In a cocktail tin, muddle the cucumber slice, then add the remaining ingredients except the beer and garnish. Wrap the rhubarb garnish around the inside of a highball glass, starting from the bottom. Fill the glass with 1¼-inch ice cubes and add the beer. Add 1¼-inch ice cubes to the cocktail tin. Cover and shake vigorously. Strain the cocktail into the highball glass.

GLASS: Highball   ICE: 1¼-inch cubes   CREATOR: Leo Robitschek

SUPERBAS

A herbaceous beer cocktail

Pilsner, Suze, Velvet Falernum, Dill, Lime

½ ounce Dill Syrup (page 228)
½ ounce John D. Taylor's Velvet Falernum
¾ ounce lime juice
1 ounce Suze
2 ounces Einbecker Pilsner
Grapefruit twist, for garnish

Combine all the ingredients except the beer and garnish in a cocktail tin.
Fill a highball glass with 1¼-inch ice cubes and add the beer. Fill the tin with
ice. Cover and shake vigorously. Strain the cocktail into the highball glass
and express the oils of the grapefruit twist over the glass. Rub the twist on
the rim of the glass and drop it into the glass, leaving the flesh side up.

GLASS: Highball   ICE: 1¼-inch cubes   CREATOR: Leo Robitschek

VELVET COBBLER

A citrus-forward summer cobbler

Amontillado Sherry, Riesling Spätlese,
Lemon Verbena

½ ounce Lemon Verbena Syrup
(page 237)
1½ ounces Riesling Spätlese
2 ounces Lustau Los Arcos
amontillado sherry
Lemon wheel, for garnish

Combine all the ingredients except the garnish in a cocktail tin. Fill
a cobbler glass with crushed ice. Add three 1¼-inch ice cubes to the tin.
Cover and whip. Strain the cocktail into the cobbler glass and garnish
with the lemon wheel.

GLASS: Cobbler   ICE: Crushed   CREATORS: Leo Robitschek
and Eamon Rockey

LIGHT
SPIRITED

18TH PARALLEL

A fruity and vegetal tiki cocktail with guava

Oaxacan Rum, Añejo Tequila, Amaro Nonino, Guava, Passionfruit, Pineapple, Cream, Lime, Vanilla, Mole Bitters

1 orange slice
4 dashes Bittermens Xocolatl Mole bitters
¼ ounce heavy cream
¼ ounce Passionfruit Syrup (page 240)
¼ ounce Vanilla Syrup (page 249)
½ ounce Guava Syrup (page 233)
½ ounce Amaro Nonino Quintessentia
½ ounce lime juice
¾ ounce pineapple juice
¾ ounce Siembra Azul añejo tequila
¾ ounce Paranubes Oaxacan rum
3 pineapple fronds, for garnish

In a cocktail tin, combine all the ingredients except the garnish. Fill a snifter with crushed ice. Add three 1¼-inch ice cubes to the cocktail tin. Cover and whip. Strain the cocktail into the snifter and top with additional crushed ice. Garnish with the pineapple fronds.

GLASS: Snifter   ICE: Crushed   CREATOR: Matt Chavez

ALL BETZ ARE OFF

A gin Old-Fashioned with celery and black pepper

London Dry Gin, Black Pepper, Demerara, Celery Bitters, Grapefruit Bitters

2 dashes Bitter Truth grapefruit bitters

4 dashes Bitter Truth celery bitters

Heavy ¼ ounce Tellicherry Black Pepper Syrup (page 248)

2 ounces Tanqueray 10 gin

Lemon twist, for garnish

Combine all the ingredients except the garnish in a mixing glass. Place a 2-inch ice cube in a double rocks glass. Fill the mixing glass with ice and stir. Strain the cocktail into the double rocks glass and express the oils of the lemon twist over the glass. Rub the twist on the rim of the glass and drop it into the glass, leaving the flesh side up.

GLASS: Double rocks   ICE: 2-inch cube   CREATOR: Jim Betz

AMELIA

A pisco sour variation with chicha morada

Pisco Quebranta, Aged Cachaça, Cream Sherry, Salers, Purple Corn, Lime, Smoked Chili Bitters, Egg White

1 egg white
6 dashes Hella Smoked Chili bitters
¼ ounce Salers Gentiane
½ ounce Lustau East India Solera cream sherry
½ ounce Avuá Amburana cachaça
¾ ounce lime juice
1 ounce Purple Corn Syrup (page 241)
1 ounce Macchu Pisco
Sombra mezcal, to finish

In a cocktail tin, combine all the ingredients except the mezcal. Seal and dry shake to emulsify the egg white into the cocktail. Carefully open the tin and fill with 1¼-inch ice cubes. Seal it again and shake vigorously. Strain the cocktail into a chilled fizz glass using a hawthorne strainer and a fine tea strainer. Using an atomizer, top with six sprays of mezcal.

GLASS: Fizz   ICE: None   CREATOR: Cristian Rodriguez

ARGYLE

A Manhattan variation with caraway and chocolate

Aged Aquavit, Marseilles Dry Vermouth, Amaro Meletti,
Maraschino, Angostura Bitters

1 dash Angostura bitters
1 teaspoon Luxardo Maraschino liqueur
½ ounce Amaro Meletti
¾ ounce Noilly Prat Extra Dry vermouth
1½ ounces Linie aquavit
Lemon twist, for garnish

Combine all the ingredients except the garnish in a mixing glass. Fill the
glass with ice and stir. Strain the cocktail into a coupe and express the oils
of the lemon twist over the glass. Rub the twist on the rim of the glass and
drop it into the glass, leaving the flesh side up.

GLASS: Coupe   ICE: None   CREATOR: Jessica Gonzalez

AVO

A spicy and savory caipirinha

Cachaça, Amaro Nonino, Aquavit, Crème de Cacao,
Jalapeño, Lemon, Orange Bitters

 4 dashes House Orange Bitters (page 234)
 ½ ounce Simple Syrup (page 245)
 ½ ounce De Kuyper crème de cacao
 ¾ ounce Krogstad aquavit
 ¾ ounce lemon juice
 ¾ ounce Amaro Nonino Quintessentia
 ¾ ounce Spicy Avuá Cachaça (page 247)
 Cacao powder, for garnish
 Mint plouche, for garnish

In a cocktail tin, combine all the ingredients except the garnishes. Fill
a Pilsner glass with crushed ice. Add three 1¼-inch ice cubes to the tin.
Cover and whip. Strain the cocktail into the Pilsner glass and top with
additional crushed ice. Garnish with cacao powder and the mint plouche.

GLASS: Pilsner   ICE: Crushed   CREATOR: Pietro Collina

BEEKEEPER

A smoky, floral gin sour

Plymouth Gin, Elderflower Liqueur, Islay Scotch, Honey, Lemon, Orange Bitters, Egg White

    1 dash House Orange Bitters (page 234)
    ¼ ounce Caol Ila 12-Year Islay Scotch
    ¼ ounce St-Germain
    ½ ounce Honey Syrup (page 233)
    ½ ounce lemon juice
    1½ ounces Plymouth gin
    1 egg white

Combine all the ingredients except the egg white in a cocktail tin. Add the egg white to the tin, cover, and dry shake to emulsify the egg white into the cocktail. Fill the tin with ice, cover again, and shake vigorously. Strain the cocktail into the coupe.

GLASS: Coupe   ICE: None   CREATOR: Lacy Hawkins

BERRY DANGEROUS FIX

A cobbler with strawberries and anise

Aquavit, Campari, Strawberry, Orange
Blossom Water, Lemon, Cane Sugar

2 Tristar strawberries, 1 for muddling
and 1 for garnish

4 drops orange blossom water

¼ ounce Campari

¾ ounce lemon juice

¾ ounce Cane Syrup (page 218)

1½ ounces Krogstad aquavit

In a cocktail tin, muddle a strawberry, then add the remaining ingredients
except the garnish. Fill a double rocks glass with crushed ice. Add three
1¼-inch ice cubes to the cocktail tin. Cover and whip. Strain the cocktail
into the double rocks glass. Fill the glass with more crushed ice and make
a mound of crushed ice up over the rim of the glass. Garnish with the
remaining strawberry.

GLASS: Double rocks   ICE: Crushed   CREATOR: Jane Danger

BLACK DAHLIA

A bitter mezcal Manhattan

Mezcal, Moscatel Sherry, Grand Marnier,
Zwack Unicum, Lemon

    1 barspoon lemon juice
    ½ ounce Zwack Unicum
    ½ ounce Grand Marnier
    ¾ ounce Moscatel
    1 ounce Sombra mezcal
    Grapefruit twist, for garnish

Combine all the ingredients except the garnish in a mixing glass. Fill the
glass with ice and stir. Strain the cocktail into a Nick and Nora glass and
express the oils of the grapefruit twist over the glass. Rub the twist on
the rim of the glass and drop it into the glass, leaving the flesh side up.

GLASS: Nick and Nora   ICE: None   CREATOR: Leo Robitschek

BLOCK PARTY

A vegetal cobbler with passionfruit

Vodka, Fino Sherry, Pale Cream Sherry, Yellow
Chartreuse, Red Pepper, Passionfruit, Vanilla, Lime

¼ ounce Vanilla Syrup (page 249)
¼ ounce Passionfruit Syrup (page 240)
½ ounce Absolut Elyx Vodka
½ ounce yellow Chartreuse
½ ounce red pepper juice
½ ounce lime juice
1 ounce Alvear Pale cream sherry
1 ounce Lustau Jarana fino sherry
3 lime wheels, for garnish
Mint plouche, for garnish

In a cocktail tin, combine all the ingredients except the garnishes. Add the
lime wheels to a Pilsner glass, going up from the base in a clockwise motion,
and then fill the glass with crushed ice. Add three 1¼-inch ice cubes to the
cocktail tin. Cover and whip. Strain the cocktail into the Pilsner glass and
top with additional crushed ice. Garnish with the mint plouche.

GLASS: Pilsner   ICE: Crushed   CREATOR: Leo Robitschek

BOHEMIA

A rich martini variation with caraway

Genever, Aquavit, Chambery Blanc Vermouth, Maraschino Liqueur

¼ ounce Luxardo Maraschino liqueur
½ ounce Krogstad aquavit
1 ounce Dolin de Chambery Blanc vermouth
1½ ounces Bols genever
Lemon twist, for garnish

Combine all the ingredients except the lemon twist in a mixing glass. Fill the glass with ice and stir. Strain the cocktail into a coupe and express the oils of the lemon twist over the glass. Rub the twist on the rim of the glass and drop it into the glass, leaving the flesh side up.

GLASS: Coupe   ICE: None   CREATOR: Leo Robitschek

BREAD AND BUTTERNUT

A festive fall cobbler reminiscent of pumpkin pie

Vodka, Cream and Amontillado Sherry, Becherovka, Kabocha Squash, Lemon, Angostura Bitters

2 dashes Angostura bitters
1 teaspoon Becherovka
½ ounce lemon juice
½ ounce Lustau Los Arcos amontillado sherry
¾ ounce Kabocha Squash Syrup (page 236)
¾ ounce Lustau East India Solera cream sherry
1 ounce Absolut Elyx vodka
1 ounce Lustau Jarana fino sherry
Lemon wheel, for garnish

In a cocktail tin, combine all the ingredients except the garnish. Fill a Pilsner glass with crushed ice. Add three 1¼-inch ice cubes to the cocktail tin. Cover and whip. Strain the cocktail into the Pilsner glass and top with additional crushed ice. Garnish with the lemon wheel.

GLASS: Pilsner   ICE: Crushed   CREATOR: Leo Robitschek

CHI CHI SWIZZLE

A caipirinha with flavors of red pepper and grapefruit

Cachaça, Amontillado Sherry, Chambery Blanc
Vermouth, Barolo Chinato, Red Bell Pepper,
Grapefruit, Lemon

1 teaspoon Cane Syrup (page 218)

½ ounce grapefruit juice

½ ounce lemon juice

½ ounce Dolin de Chambery Blanc vermouth

¾ ounce Lustau Los Arcos amontillado sherry

1 ounce Novo Fogo cachaça

1½ ounces Red Bell Pepper and Thai Bird
Chile–Infused Barolo Chinato (page 242)

Horse's neck lemon twist, for garnish

Combine all the ingredients except the lemon twist in a cocktail tin. Fill
a Pilsner glass with crushed ice. Add three 1¼-inch ice cubes to the tin.
Cover and whip. Strain the cocktail into the Pilsner glass, twist the horse's
neck lemon twist into a tight coil, and lay it on top of the glass.

GLASS: Pilsner   ICE: Crushed   CREATOR: Will Peet

CHOKED UP

A bitter gin sour with kumquat

London Dry Gin, Cynar, Kumquat, Cucumber, Mint, Lemon, Salt

Lemon wedge, for rimming
Salt, for rimming
1 kumquat, cut in half, ½ for muddling and ½ for garnish
2 cucumber slices, 1 for muddling and 1 for garnish
5 mint leaves
5 drops Saline Solution (page 245)
½ ounce Cane Syrup (page 218)
¾ ounce lemon juice
1 ounce Cynar
1 ounce Beefeater gin
Mint plouche, for garnish

Use the lemon wedge to moisten the top inch of the outer rim of a chilled double rocks glass. Gently roll the double rocks glass in salt to rim half of the glass. Shake off excess salt. Use the corner of a folded cocktail napkin to make the salt a consistent thickness. In a cocktail tin, muddle a kumquat half, a cucumber slice, and the mint leaves, then add the remaining ingredients except the garnishes. Fill the double rocks glass with 1¼-inch ice cubes. Fill the cocktail tin with 1¼-inch ice cubes. Cover and shake vigorously. Strain the cocktail into the double rocks glass. Garnish with the mint plouche and remaining cucumber slice and kumquat half.

GLASS: Double rocks   ICE: 1¼-inch cubes   CREATOR: Leo Robitschek

COQ-TAIL #1

A bright, floral vodka sour

Vodka, Chambery Blanc Vermouth, Elderflower Liqueur,
Absinthe, Honey, Pineapple, Lemon

SERVES 2

- 1 barspoon yuzu juice
- 1 teaspoon Vieux Pontarlier absinthe verte
- 1 ounce lemon juice
- 1 ounce pineapple juice
- 1 ounce Honey Syrup (page 233)
- 1 ounce St-Germain
- 1 ounce Dolin de Chambery Blanc vermouth
- 3 ounces Absolut Elyx vodka

In a cocktail tin, combine all the ingredients. Fill a rooster cup with
crushed ice. Add three 1¼-inch ice cubes to the cocktail tin. Cover
and whip vigorously. Strain the cocktail into the rooster cup using
a hawthorne strainer and top with additional crushed ice.

GLASS: Rooster   ICE: Crushed   CREATOR: Leo Robitschek

COQ-TAIL #2

A buttery, herbaceous vodka sour

Vodka, Chambery Blanc Vermouth, Pear Brandy, Falernum,
Brown Butter, Black Pepper, Tarragon, Yuzu

SERVES 2

  4 dashes yuzu juice
  15 tarragon leaves
  Scant 1 ounce Brown Butter Falernum (page 218)
  1 ounce lemon juice
  1 ounce Tellicherry Black Pepper Syrup (page 248)
  1 ounce Clear Creek Pear brandy
  2 ounces Dolin de Chambery Blanc vermouth
  2 ounces Absolut Elyx vodka

In a cocktail tin, combine all the ingredients. Fill a rooster cup with
crushed ice. Add three 1¼-inch ice cubes to the cocktail tin. Cover
and whip vigorously. Strain the cocktail into the rooster cup using
a hawthorne strainer and top with additional crushed ice.

GLASS: Rooster   ICE: Crushed   CREATORS: Nathan O'Neill,
                                              Pietro Collina, and Leo Robitschek

COQ-TAIL #3

A silky vodka sour with corn

Vodka, Amontillado Sherry, Corn, Cinnamon, Yuzu, Lime

SERVES 2

Scant ½ ounce yuzu juice

Scant ½ ounce Ceylon Cinnamon Syrup (page 219)

1 ounce lime juice

2 ounces Lustau Los Arcos amontillado sherry

2 ounces Corn Syrup (page 227)

2 ounces Absolut Elyx vodka

In a cocktail tin, combine all the ingredients. Fill a rooster cup with crushed ice. Add three 1¼-inch ice cubes to the cocktail tin. Cover and whip vigorously. Strain the cocktail into the rooster cup using a hawthorne strainer and top with additional crushed ice.

GLASS: Rooster   ICE: Crushed   CREATORS: Nathan O'Neill, Pietro Collina, and Leo Robitschek

DELI SLANG

A gin sour inspired by the flavors of a delicatessen

London Dry Gin, Suze, Lemon Verbena, Buttermilk, Horseradish, Lemon, Egg White

1 egg white

6 drops Horseradish Tincture (page 234), plus 4 dashes, for garnish

1 teaspoon Suze

¼ ounce Agave Syrup (page 216)

¾ ounce lemon juice

1 ounce Lemon Verbena–Infused Buttermilk (page 237)

1½ ounces Beefeater gin

In a cocktail tin, combine all the ingredients except the garnish. Seal and dry shake to emulsify the egg white into the cocktail. Carefully open the tin and fill with 1¼-inch ice cubes. Seal it again and shake vigorously.

Strain the cocktail into a chilled coupe using a hawthorne strainer and a fine tea strainer. Once the egg white settles, use a Japanese bitters dasher to carefully add dots of horseradish tincture around the rim of the glass.

GLASS: Coupe   ICE: None   CREATOR: Leo Robitschek

DEWIN' IT

A spicy margarita with roasted poblano peppers
———

Jalapeño-Infused Tequila, Mezcal, Suze, Roasted Poblano Pepper, Vanilla, Lemon

   ½ ounce Roasted Poblano Pepper Syrup (page 244)
   ½ ounce Vanilla Syrup (page 249)
   ¾ ounce lemon juice
   ¾ ounce Suze
   ¾ ounce Jalapeño-Infused Tequila (page 235)
   ¾ ounce Sombra mezcal

In a cocktail tin, combine all the ingredients. Fill a Pilsner glass with crushed ice. Add three 1¼-inch ice cubes to the cocktail tin. Cover and whip. Strain the cocktail into the Pilsner glass and top with additional crushed ice.

GLASS: Pilsner   ICE: Crushed   CREATOR: Leo Robitschek

DR. FEELGOOD

A velvety mezcal margarita with spice

Mezcal, Fino Sherry, Suze, Génépy, Avocado, Lemon,
Cucumber, Jalapeño, Salt, Aleppo Chile

Lime wedge, for rimming

Aleppo chile salt, for rimming

Cucumber slice, for muddling, plus
whole-length cucumber slice, for garnish

¼ ounce Jalapeño-Infused Agave Syrup (page 235)

¼ ounce Dolin Génépy

½ ounce lemon juice

½ ounce Suze

¾ ounce Avocado Syrup (page 216)

¾ ounce Lustau Jarana fino sherry

1 ounce Sombra mezcal

2 pineapple fronds, for garnish

Use the lime wedge to moisten the top inch of the outer rim of a chilled
double rocks glass. Gently roll the double rocks glass in chile salt to rim
half of the glass. Shake off excess salt. Use the corner of a folded cocktail
napkin to make the salt a consistent thickness. In a cocktail tin, muddle a
cucumber slice, then add the remaining ingredients except the garnishes.
Fill the double rocks glass with 1¼-inch ice cubes. Fill the cocktail tin with
1¼-inch ice cubes. Cover and shake vigorously. Strain the cocktail into the
double rocks glass. Take the remaining cucumber slice and roll it tight.
Skewer the cucumber and two small tips of the pineapple fronds and
garnish the cocktail.

GLASS: Double rocks   ICE: 1¼-inch cubes   CREATOR: Leo Robitschek

DR. WALNUT

A nutty and bitter gin sour

———

Genever, Amaro Ciociaro, Frangelico, Royal Combier,
Ginger, Lemon, Egg White

1 egg white
¼ ounce Royal Combier
¼ ounce Frangelico
½ ounce lemon juice
½ ounce Ginger Lime Syrup (page 231)
¾ ounce Paolucci Amaro Ciociaro
1 ounce Bols genever
Shaved hazelnut, for garnish
Shaved walnut, for garnish

In a cocktail tin, combine all the ingredients except the garnishes. Seal
and dry shake to emulsify the egg white into the cocktail. Carefully open
the tin and fill with 1¼-inch ice cubes. Seal it again and shake vigorously.
Strain the cocktail into a chilled coupe using a hawthorne strainer and
a fine tea strainer. Garnish with hazelnut and walnut shavings.

GLASS: Coupe   ICE: None   CREATOR: Nathan O'Neill

EL REY

A tequila cobbler with the flavors of seasonal Mexican corn

———

Highlands Blanco Tequila, Amontillado Sherry, Corn, Coconut, Lime, Pistachio

¼ ounce Coconut Syrup (page 225)
½ ounce lime juice
½ ounce Excellia Blanco tequila
1 ounce Corn Syrup (page 227)
1½ ounces Lustau Los Arcos amontillado sherry
Lime zest, for garnish
Shaved pistachio, for garnish

In a cocktail tin, combine all the ingredients except the garnishes. Fill a highball glass with crushed ice. Add three 1¼-inch ice cubes to the cocktail tin. Cover and whip vigorously. Strain the cocktail into the highball glass and top with additional crushed ice. Garnish with zested lime and pistachio shavings.

GLASS: Highball   ICE: Crushed   CREATOR: Leo Robitschek

EL TUCAN

A smoky, vegetal paloma

Mezcal, Genepy, Celery, Grapefruit, Agave,
Peychaud's Bitters, Salt

> 2 lime wedges, 1 for rimming and 1 for garnish
> Salt, for rimming
> ½ ounce Agave Syrup (page 216)
> ½ ounce grapefruit juice
> ½ ounce celery juice
> ¾ ounce lime juice
> 1 ounce Alpe Genepy
> 1 ounce Sombra mezcal
> 4 dashes Peychaud's bitters, for garnish
> 1 ounce Seagram's club soda

Use a lime wedge to moisten the top inch of the outer rim of a chilled
highball glass. Gently roll the highball glass in salt to rim half of the glass.
Shake off excess salt. Use the corner of a folded cocktail napkin to make
the salt a consistent thickness. Fill the highball glass with 1¼-inch ice
cubes. In a cocktail tin, combine the remaining ingredients except the
garnishes and club soda. Add three 1¼-inch ice cubes to the tin. Seal the
tin and whip vigorously. Strain the cocktail into the highball glass using
a hawthorne strainer. Add the Peychaud's bitters to the top of the drink
and then fill the glass with the club soda and garnish with the remaining
lime wedge.

GLASS: Highball   ICE: 1¼-inch cubes   CREATOR: Leo Robitschek

ENGLISH HEAT

A spicy gin sour with hints of vanilla

London Dry Gin, Chambery Dry Vermouth,
Tuaca, Jalapeño, Agave, Lemon

¼ ounce Tuaca
¾ ounce Jalapeño-Infused
Agave Syrup (page 235)
¾ ounce Dolin de Chambery Dry vermouth
1 ounce lemon juice
1½ ounces Beefeater gin

Combine all the ingredients in a cocktail tin. Fill a fizz glass with 1¼-inch
ice cubes. Fill the tin with ice, cover, and shake vigorously. Strain the
cocktail into the fizz glass.

GLASS: Fizz   ICE: 1¼-inch cubes   CREATOR: Leo Robitschek

FAR FROM THE TREE

A fall-spiced margarita with hints of apple

Highlands Blanco Tequila, Pommeau, Cardamaro, Allspice Dram,
Lemon, Cinnamon, Mole Bitters

4 dashes Bittermens Xocolatl Mole bitters
½ ounce Cassia Cinnamon Syrup (page 218)
¾ ounce lemon juice
¾ ounce Cardamaro
¾ ounce Camut Pommeau
1 ounce Excellia Blanco tequila
St. Elizabeth allspice dram, as a rinse

Combine all the ingredients except the allspice dram in a cocktail tin.
Rinse a double rocks glass with six sprays of allspice dram from an
atomizer and place a 2-inch ice cube in it. Fill the tin with ice, cover,
and shake. Strain the cocktail into the glass.

GLASS: Double rocks   ICE: 2-inch ice cube   CREATOR: Leo Robitschek

FIG AND THISTLE

A fig-and-honey-flavored tequila sour

Highlands Blanco Tequila, Cardamaro, Fig Leaf, Honey, Earl Grey, Lemon, Aromatic Bitters, Salt

2 dashes Bitter Truth aromatic bitters
5 drops Saline Solution (page 245)
1 teaspoon Honey Syrup (page 233)
Scant ½ ounce lemon juice
½ ounce Fig Leaf Syrup (page 230)
1 ounce Cardamaro
1½ ounces Earl Grey Tea-Washed Excellia Blanco Tequila (page 229)

In a cocktail tin, combine all the ingredients. Cover and dry shake vigorously. Fill a double rocks glass with 1¼-inch ice cubes. Fill the cocktail tin with 1¼-inch ice cubes. Seal it again and shake vigorously. Strain the cocktail into the double rocks glass.

GLASS: Double rocks   ICE: 1¼-inch cubes   CREATOR: Leo Robitschek

FORBIDDEN DANCE

A tiki drink with caraway and malt

———

Aquavit, Genever, Velvet Falernum, Amontillado Sherry, Orgeat,
Vanilla, Pineapple, Lime

¼ ounce Vanilla Syrup (page 249)
¼ ounce John D. Taylor's Velvet Falernum
½ ounce lime juice
½ ounce pineapple juice
½ ounce Orgeat (page 239)
¾ ounce Lustau Los Arcos amontillado sherry
1 ounce Bols genever
1 ounce Krogstad aquavit
Mint plouche, for garnish
Grated nutmeg, for garnish

Combine all the ingredients except the mint and nutmeg in a cocktail
tin. Fill a tiki mug with crushed ice. Add three 1¼-inch ice cubes to the
tin, cover, and whip. Strain the cocktail into the tiki mug and top with
additional crushed ice. Garnish with the mint plouche and grated nutmeg.

GLASS: Tiki mug   ICE: Crushed   CREATOR: Wally Suarez

THE GILSEY

A savory, vegetal martini

London Dry Gin, Pale Cream Sherry, Cocchi Americano, Kirschwasser, Green Chartreuse, Orange Bitters

1 dash House Orange Bitters (page 234)

1 teaspoon Clear Creek kirschwasser

½ ounce Cocchi Americano

¾ ounce Alvear Pale cream sherry

¾ ounce Tanqueray gin

¾ ounce Tanqueray 10 gin

Green Chartreuse, as a rinse

Combine all the ingredients except the Chartreuse in a mixing glass. Rinse a coupe with six sprays of green Chartreuse from an atomizer. Fill the mixing glass with ice and stir. Strain the cocktail into the coupe.

GLASS: Coupe   ICE: None   CREATOR: Jessica Gonzalez

GOLDEN TICKET

A margarita with flavors of mole

Highlands Blanco Tequila, Pale Cream Sherry, Ancho Reyes,
Crème de Cacao, Lemon, Chocolate

3 dashes Bitter Truth chocolate bitters

1 teaspoon Marie Brizard crème de cacao

¼ ounce Agave Syrup (page 216)

½ ounce lemon juice

½ ounce Ancho Reyes

1 ounce Alvear Pale cream sherry

1 ounce Excellia Blanco tequila

Chocolate Shell (page 223), for garnish

In a cocktail tin, combine all the ingredients except the garnish. Using
a brush, paint a brushstroke of chocolate shell in a chilled double rocks
glass, starting at the bottom and going to the top in a 45-degree angle.
Place a 2-inch ice cube in the double rocks glass. Fill the cocktail tin
with 1¼-inch ice cubes. Seal the tin and shake. Strain the cocktail into
the double rocks glass using a hawthorne strainer and a fine tea strainer.

GLASS: Double rocks   ICE: 2-inch cube   CREATOR: Nathan O'Neill

GREEN STREETS

A lighter, vegetal pisco Negroni

Pisco Acholado, Chambery Blanc Vermouth, Cocchi Americano, Sorrel

1 ounce Cocchi Americano
1 ounce Sorrel-Infused Dolin de Chambery Blanc Vermouth (page 246)
1 ounce Macchu Pisco La Diablada
Sorrel leaf, for garnish

In a chilled mixing glass, combine all the ingredients except the garnish. Fill the mixing glass with 1¼-inch ice cubes and stir. Strain the cocktail into a chilled double rocks glass over a 2-inch ice cube. Garnish with the sorrel leaf.

GLASS: Double rocks   ICE: 2-inch cube   CREATOR: Leo Robitschek

HEARSAY

A fall-spiced mezcal Manhattan

Mezcal, Amaro Nonino, Moscatel Sherry, Jamaican Rum, Pimento Dram, Grapefruit Bitters

1 dash Bitter Truth grapefruit bitters
1 teaspoon Hamilton pimento dram
¼ ounce Hamilton Jamaican gold rum
½ ounce Lustau Emilín Moscatel sherry
¾ ounce Amaro Nonino Quintessentia
1 ounce Del Maguey Vida mezcal

In a mixing glass, combine all the ingredients. Fill the mixing glass with 1¼-inch ice cubes and stir. Strain the cocktail into a Nick and Nora glass using a hawthorne strainer.

GLASS: Nick and Nora   ICE: None   CREATOR: Nathan O'Neill

HONEY OAT

A milk-and-honey-flavored Ramos gin fizz

Brandy, Honey Liqueur, Yellow Chartreuse, Oolong Tea, Lemon, Oatmilk

1 egg white
4 dashes Pernod Absinthe
¼ ounce yellow Chartreuse
½ ounce KAS Krupnikas
¾ ounce Oolong Syrup (page 239)
¾ ounce lemon juice
¾ ounce Oatly oatmilk
1 ounce Monteru brandy

In a cocktail tin, combine all the ingredients. Seal and dry shake to emulsify the egg white into the cocktail. Carefully open the tin and fill with 1¼-inch ice cubes. Seal it again and shake vigorously. Strain the cocktail into a chilled fizz glass using a hawthorne strainer and a fine tea strainer.

GLASS: Fizz   ICE: None   CREATOR: Pietro Collina

HOT LIPS

A take on a smoky-spicy margarita with pineapple and vanilla

Jalapeño-Infused Blanco Tequila, Mezcal,
Pineapple, Vanilla

1 teaspoon Cane Syrup (page 218)
½ ounce Vanilla Syrup (page 249)
½ ounce pineapple juice
¾ ounce Sombra mezcal
¾ ounce Jalapeño-Infused Tequila (page 235)
Salt, for rimming

Combine all the ingredients except the salt in a mixing glass. Rim a single rocks glass with salt and fill it with 1¼-inch ice cubes. Fill the mixing glass with ice and stir. Strain the cocktail into the single rocks glass.

GLASS: Single rocks   ICE: 1¼-inch cubes   CREATOR: Jessica Gonzalez

ISLAND TIME

A tiki cocktail with ginger and peach

Panamanian Rum, Antiguan Rum, Crème de Pêche, Suze, Orgeat,
Ginger, Lime, Orange Bitters

2 dashes House Orange Bitters (page 234)
1 teaspoon Spicy Ginger Syrup (page 247)
½ ounce Massenez Crème de Pêche
½ ounce English Harbour rum
½ ounce Suze
½ ounce grapefruit juice
¾ ounce lime juice
¾ ounce Orgeat (page 239)
1 ounce Caña Brava rum
6 dashes Angostura bitters, for garnish
Mint plouche, for garnish

In a cocktail tin, combine all the ingredients except the garnishes. Fill a
Pilsner glass with crushed ice. Add three 1¼-inch ice cubes to the cocktail
tin. Cover and whip. Strain the cocktail into the Pilsner glass, add the
Angostura bitters, and top with additional crushed ice. Garnish with
the mint plouche.

GLASS: Pilsner   ICE: Crushed   CREATOR: Guillermo Bravo

JITNEY

A mezcal Negroni variation with coffee and absinthe

Mezcal, Campari, Marseilles Dry Vermouth,
Chambery Blanc Vermouth, Coffee, Absinthe

2 dashes Pernod Absinthe
½ ounce Coffee-Infused Dry Vermouth (page 226)
½ ounce Dolin de Chambery Blanc vermouth
¾ ounce Campari
¾ ounce Sombra mezcal
Grapefruit twist, for garnish

Combine all the ingredients except the grapefruit twist in a mixing glass.
Add a 2-inch ice cube to a double rocks glass. Fill the mixing glass with
ice and stir. Strain the cocktail into the double rocks glass and express
the oils of the grapefruit twist over the glass. Rub the twist on the rim
of the glass and drop it into the glass, leaving the flesh side up.

GLASS: Double rocks   ICE: 2-inch cube   CREATOR: Leo Robitschek

KOALA PEAR

A Tom Collins with eucalyptus and bay leaf

New American Gin, Pear Brandy, Cocchi Americano,
Eucalyptus, Bay Leaf, Lemon

¾ ounce lemon juice
¾ ounce Cocchi Americano
1 ounce Eucalyptus Bay Leaf Syrup (page 229)
1 ounce Purkhart Pear Williams brandy
1 ounce St. George Terroir gin
1 ounce Seagram's club soda
2 lemon wheels, for garnish
Bay leaf, for garnish

In a cocktail tin, combine all the ingredients except the club soda and
garnishes. Fill a highball glass with 1¼-inch ice cubes. Fill the cocktail tin
with 1¼-inch ice cubes. Cover and shake vigorously. Add the club soda

to the cocktail tin. Strain the cocktail into the highball glass. Skewer the lemon wheels, one on top of the other, and put the bay leaf between them, then garnish the cocktail.

GLASS: Highball   ICE: 1¼-inch cubes   CREATOR: Pietro Collina

LOISAIDA AVENUE

A mezcal margarita that is spicy and herbaceous

Mezcal, Tequila, Green Chartreuse,
Jalapeño, Lemon, Angostura Bitters

½ ounce Simple Syrup (page 245)
½ ounce green Chartreuse
¾ ounce lemon juice
¾ ounce Sombra mezcal
¾ ounce Jalapeño-Infused Tequila (page 235)
1 dash Angostura bitters, for garnish

Combine all the ingredients except the bitters in a cocktail tin. Fill the tin with ice, cover, and shake vigorously. Strain the cocktail into a Nick and Nora glass. Top the cocktail with the Angostura bitters.

GLASS: Nick and Nora   ICE: None   CREATOR: Leo Robitschek

LONGFELLOW

A Tom Collins with horseradish and apple

Plymouth Gin, Cocchi Americano, Apple Brandy, Pear Brandy,
Honey, Cinnamon, Horseradish, Lemon, Cardamom, Absinthe

2 cardamom pods, for muddling

4 dashes Pernod Absinthe

4 drops Saline Solution (page 245)

¼ ounce Clear Creek Pear brandy

¼ ounce Ceylon Cinnamon Syrup (page 219)

½ ounce Honey Syrup (page 233)

½ ounce St. George unaged apple brandy

¾ ounce lemon juice

¾ ounce Cocchi Americano

1½ ounces Horseradish-Infused Gin
(page 233)

1 ounce Seagram's club soda

Daikon radish, for garnish

In a cocktail tin, muddle the cardamom pods, then add the remaining
ingredients except the club soda and garnish. Fill a black highball glass
with 1¼-inch ice cubes. Fill the cocktail tin with 1¼-inch ice cubes. Cover
and shake vigorously. Add the club soda to the tin. Strain the cocktail
into the highball glass. Using a vegetable sheeter, sheet a foot of daikon
radish. Fold the radish lengthwise into a fan, so it looks like a flower, and
insert it into the top of the glass.

GLASS: Black highball by Stölzle   ICE: 1¼-inch cubes   CREATOR: Nathan O'Neill

LOWRIDER

A mezcal Manhattan with fig

Mezcal, Moscatel and Oloroso Sherry, Amaro Nonino, Fig,
Verjus, Aromatic Bitters

1 dash Bitter Truth aromatic bitters
6 dashes Angostura bitters
1 teaspoon Fusion verjus blanc juice
¼ ounce Fig Leaf Syrup (page 230)
¼ ounce Lustau Don Nuño Oloroso sherry
½ ounce Amaro Nonino Quintessentia
½ ounce Lustau Emilín Moscatel sherry
1 ounce Sombra mezcal

In a chilled mixing glass, combine all the ingredients. Fill the mixing glass
with 1¼-inch ice cubes and stir. Strain the cocktail into a chilled double
rocks glass over a 2-inch ice cube.

GLASS: Double rocks   ICE: 2-inch cube   CREATOR: Leo Robitschek

MAD GNOME

A dirty chai vodka cobbler

Vodka, Marseilles Vermouth, Pale Cream Sherry,
Vermouth di Torino, Chai, Coffee, Absinthe, Lemon

3 dashes Pernod Absinthe

½ ounce Cane Syrup (page 218)

½ ounce lemon juice

½ ounce Chai-Infused Cocchi
Vermouth di Torino (page 220)

½ ounce Absolut Elyx vodka

½ ounce Alvear Pale cream sherry

½ ounce Coffee-Infused Dry Vermouth (page 226)

In a cocktail tin, combine all the ingredients. Fill a copper gnome glass
or a chilled double rocks glass with 1¼-inch ice cubes. Fill the cocktail tin
with 1¼-inch ice cubes. Seal the tin and shake. Strain the cocktail into the
gnome glass using a hawthorne strainer and a fine tea strainer.

GLASS: Copper gnome
or double rocks

ICE: 1¼-inch cubes

CREATORS: Leo Robitschek
and Pietro Collina

MAIZE RUNNER

A corn-and-blueberry cobbler

Genever, Amontillado Sherry, Corn, Coconut, Lime, Blueberries

    5 blueberries, for muddling
    ¼ ounce Coconut Syrup (page 225)
    ½ ounce lime juice
    ½ ounce Bols genever
    1 ounce Corn Syrup (page 227)
    1½ ounces Lustau Los Arcos amontillado sherry
    Lime zest, for garnish
    Orange zest, for garnish

In a cocktail tin, muddle the blueberries, then add the remaining
ingredients except the garnishes. Fill a highball glass with crushed
ice. Add three 1¼-inch ice cubes to the cocktail tin. Cover and whip
vigorously. Strain the cocktail into the highball glass and top with
additional crushed ice. Garnish with lime and orange zests.

GLASS: Highball   ICE: Crushed   CREATOR: Shaun Dunn

MOTHER'S LITTLE HELPER

A floral-rich gin martini

Genever, Pale Cream Sherry, Chambery Dry Vermouth,
Triple Sec, Elderflower Liqueur

    1 dash Peychaud's bitters
    1 teaspoon St-Germain
    ½ ounce Combier triple sec
    ¾ ounce Dolin de Chambery Dry vermouth
    1 ounce Alvear Pale cream sherry
    1 ounce Bols genever

Combine all the ingredients in a mixing glass. Fill the mixing glass with
ice and stir. Strain the cocktail into a coupe.

GLASS: Coupe   ICE: None   CREATOR: Jessica Gonzalez

NEEDLE AND THREAD

A citrus-forward gin martini

London Dry Gin, Gentiane, Chambery Blanc Vermouth,
Acqua di Cedro, Orange Bitters, Absinthe

2 dashes House Orange Bitters (page 234)

½ ounce Nardini Acqua di Cedro

½ ounce Salers Gentiane

½ ounce Dolin de Chambery Blanc vermouth

2 ounces Beefeater gin

Pernod Absinthe, as a rinse

Lemon twist, for expressing

Combine all the ingredients except the absinthe and lemon twist
in a mixing glass. Rinse a coupe glass with six sprays of absinthe
from an atomizer. Fill the mixing glass with ice and stir. Strain
the cocktail into the coupe. Express the oils of the lemon twist
over the glass, then discard the twist.

GLASS: Coupe   ICE: None   CREATORS: Will Peet
                                                     and Leo Robitschek

NOD TO NOTHING

A floral, tart, and herbaceous gin fix

London Dry Gin, Cocchi Americano, Apricot Liqueur,
Jasmine, Yuzu, Lemon, Sage

    5 sage leaves
    3 dashes yuzu juice
    ¼ ounce Marie Brizard Apry
    ½ ounce Jasmine Pearl Syrup (page 235)
    ¾ ounce lemon juice
    ¾ ounce Cocchi Americano
    1 ounce Fords gin
    Lemon wheel, for garnish

In a cocktail tin, combine all the ingredients except the garnish. Fill a
double rocks glass with crushed ice. Add three 1¼-inch ice cubes to the
cocktail tin. Cover and whip. Strain the cocktail into the double rocks
glass, add additional crushed ice, and dome the top of the cocktail using
a julep strainer. Garnish with the lemon wheel.

GLASS: Double rocks   ICE: Crushed   CREATOR: Leo Robitschek

OLD RANHOFER

A spicy rum Old-Fashioned with flavors of rum raisin

Haitian Rum, Raisin, Vanilla, Coffee, Jamaican Jerk Bitters

    2 dashes The Bitter End Jamaican Jerk bitters
    1 barspoon Cold Brew Coffee Concentrate (page 226)
    Heavy ¼ ounce Vanilla Syrup (page 249)
    2 ounces Raisin-Infused Barbancourt Blanc Rhum (page 241)

In a mixing glass, combine all the ingredients. Place a 2-inch ice cube in
a double rocks glass. Fill the mixing glass with 1¼-inch ice cubes and stir.
Strain the cocktail into the double rocks glass.

GLASS: Double rocks   ICE: 2-inch cube   CREATOR: Jim Betz

PAINT IT BLACK

A tequila cobbler with blackberries and vanilla

Highlands Blanco Tequila, Fino Sherry,
Velvet Falernum, Vanilla, Blackberries

¼ ounce Vanilla Syrup (page 249)
½ ounce John D. Taylor's Velvet Falernum
¾ ounce lemon juice
1 ounce Lustau Jarana fino sherry
1 ounce Excellia Blanco Tequila
¼ ounce Simple Syrup (page 245)
5 medium blackberries, for muddling

In a cocktail tin, combine all the ingredients except the simple syrup and
blackberries. Fill a highball glass with crushed ice. In a separate cocktail
tin, combine the simple syrup and blackberries and muddle. Add three
1¼-inch ice cubes to the tin with the liquid ingredients. Cover and whip.
Strain the cocktail into the highball glass and top with additional crushed
ice and the muddled blackberry mixture.

GLASS: Highball   ICE: Crushed   CREATORS: Jessica Gonzalez
                                                     and Leo Robitschek

PANAMERICANO

A white Negroni variation highlighting pisco

Pisco Quebranta, Chambery Blanc Vermouth, Cocchi Americano

1 ounce Dolin de Chambery Blanc vermouth
1 ounce Cocchi Americano
1 ounce Macchu Pisco
Orange twist, for garnish

Combine all the ingredients except the orange twist in a mixing glass.
Place a 2-inch ice cube in a double rocks glass. Fill the mixing glass with
ice and stir. Strain the cocktail into the double rocks glass and express
the oils of the orange twist over the glass. Rub the twist on the rim of the
glass and drop it into the glass, leaving the flesh side up.

GLASS: Double rocks   ICE: 2-inch cube   CREATOR: Leo Robitschek

PARIS IS BURNING

A smoky gin sour with elderflower

London Dry Gin, Mezcal, Elderflower Liqueur,
Pineapple, Lemon, Angostura Bitters

¼ ounce Cane Syrup (page 218)
½ ounce St-Germain
½ ounce lemon juice
1 ounce pineapple juice
1 ounce Sombra mezcal
1 ounce Beefeater gin
1 dash Angostura bitters, for garnish

Combine all the ingredients except the bitters in a cocktail tin.
Fill the tin with ice. Cover and shake. Strain the cocktail into a coupe.
Top with the Angostura bitters.

GLASS: Coupe   ICE: None   CREATOR: Leo Robitschek

PETTICOAT

A gin sour with Szechuan spice

London Dry Gin, Velvet Falernum, Apricot Liqueur,
Szechuan Peppercorn, Lemon

   ¼ ounce Cane Syrup (page 218)
   ¼ ounce John D. Taylor's Velvet Falernum
   ¼ ounce Marie Brizard Apry
   ½ ounce lemon juice
   2 ounces Szechuan Peppercorn–Infused Gin (page 248)

Combine all the ingredients in a cocktail tin. Fill the tin with ice, cover,
and shake. Strain the cocktail into a coupe.

GLASS: Coupe   ICE: None   CREATOR: Jessica Gonzalez

PIEDMONT FIZZ

An anise-forward gin Collins

London Dry Gin, Cocchi Americano,
Absinthe, Lemon

   ½ ounce Simple Syrup (page 245)
   ¾ ounce lemon juice
   1 ounce Cocchi Americano
   1 ounce Beefeater gin
   1 ounce Seagram's club soda
   ¼ ounce Pernod Absinthe, to float
   Lemon wheel, for garnish

Combine the simple syrup, lemon juice, Cocchi Americano, and gin
in a cocktail tin. Fill a highball glass with 1¼-inch ice cubes. Fill the
cocktail tin with ice, cover, and shake vigorously. Strain the cocktail
into the highball glass. Add the club soda and float the absinthe on
top of the drink. Garnish with the lemon wheel.

GLASS: Highball   ICE: 1¼-inch cubes   CREATOR: Leo Robitschek

RAINBOW ROAD

A herbaceous, stone-fruit highball

Pisco Acholado, Crème de Pêche, Strega, Lemon, Honey, Basil, Peychaud's Bitters

  3 basil leaves
  ¼ ounce Honey Syrup (page 233)
  ¼ ounce Strega
  ½ ounce Massenez Crème de Pêche
  ¾ ounce lemon juice
  1 ounce Macchu Pisco La Diablada
  6 dashes Peychaud's bitters, for garnish
  Lime wheel, for garnish

In a cocktail tin, combine all the ingredients except the garnishes. Fill a highball glass with crushed ice. Add three 1¼-inch ice cubes to the cocktail tin. Cover and whip. Strain the cocktail into the highball glass, add the Peychaud's bitters, and top with additional crushed ice. Garnish with the lime wheel.

GLASS: Highball   ICE: Crushed   CREATOR: Pietro Collina

RED LIGHT

A bittered anise–flavored daiquiri

Nicaraguan Rum, Aquavit, Campari, Velvet Falernum,
Vanilla, Grapefruit, Lime, Wormwood Bitters

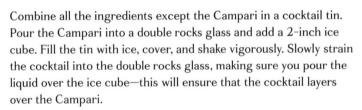

2 dashes Cocktail Kingdom Wormwood bitters
¼ ounce John D. Taylor's Velvet Falernum
½ ounce Vanilla Syrup (page 249)
½ ounce lime juice
¾ ounce ruby red grapefruit juice
1 ounce Flor de Caña 4-Year Extra Dry rum
1 ounce Krogstad aquavit
½ ounce Campari

Combine all the ingredients except the Campari in a cocktail tin.
Pour the Campari into a double rocks glass and add a 2-inch ice
cube. Fill the tin with ice, cover, and shake vigorously. Slowly strain
the cocktail into the double rocks glass, making sure you pour the
liquid over the ice cube—this will ensure that the cocktail layers
over the Campari.

GLASS: Double rocks   ICE: 2-inch cube   CREATOR: Jessica Gonzalez

RED PEPPER–PASSIONFRUIT DAIQUIRI

A savory daiquiri that is perfect for brunch

Antiguan Rum, Jamaican Rum, Guyanese Rum, Passionfruit,
Red Pepper, Honey, Lemon

2 dashes Angostura bitters
¼ ounce Passionfruit Syrup (page 240)
½ ounce El Dorado 15-Year rum
½ ounce Appleton Signature rum
Scant ¾ ounce Red Pepper Honey Syrup (page 243)
¾ ounce lemon juice
1 ounce English Harbour rum

In a cocktail tin, combine all the ingredients. Fill the tin with 1¼-inch ice cubes. Cover and shake. Strain the cocktail into a chilled coupe.

GLASS: Coupe   ICE: None   CREATOR: Leo Robitschek

RUE BARBARE

A smoky rhubarb–olive oil tequila sour

Highlands Blanco Tequila, Fino Sherry, Crema de Mezcal, Rhubarb,
Lemon, Olive Oil, Angostura Bitters, Peychaud's Bitters

2 mint leaves
2 dashes Angostura bitters
2 dashes Peychaud's bitters
½ ounce Del Maguey Crema de Mezcal
¾ ounce lemon juice
¾ ounce Rhubarb Syrup (page 244)
1 ounce Lustau Jarana fino sherry
1 ounce Olive Oil–Washed Tequila (page 239)
Sombra mezcal, to finish

Combine all the ingredients except the mezcal in a cocktail tin. Fill the tin with ice, cover, and shake. Strain into a double rocks glass over a 2-inch ice cube. Top with six sprays of mezcal from an atomizer.

GLASS: Double rocks   ICE: 2-inch cube   CREATOR: Leo Robitschek

RUNYON CANYON

A tiki variation on the flavors of a vodka cranberry

Vodka, Vermouth di Torino, Amontillado Sherry, Cranberry, Passionfruit, Lime, Mint, Islay Scotch

¼ ounce Cane Syrup (page 218)
¼ ounce Passionfruit Syrup (page 240)
½ ounce Cranberry Syrup (page 227)
½ ounce lime juice
¾ ounce Lustau Los Arcos amontillado sherry
¾ ounce Cocchi Vermouth di Torino
1½ ounces Absolut Elyx vodka
Mint plouche, for garnish
Laphroaig 10-Year Scotch, for garnish

In a cocktail tin, combine all the ingredients except the garnishes. Fill a Belgium glass with crushed ice. Add three 1¼-inch ice cubes to the cocktail tin. Cover and whip vigorously. Strain the cocktail into the Belgium glass using a hawthorne strainer and top with additional crushed ice. Using an atomizer, spritz the mint plouche with six sprays of Scotch and garnish the cocktail.

GLASS: Belgium   ICE: Crushed   CREATOR: Shaun Dunn

SAKURA MARU

A pisco sour with cinnamon and yogurt

Genever, Pisco Quebranta, Aged Cachaça, Green Tea,
Sheep's Milk Yogurt, Lemon

  ½ ounce Agave Syrup (page 216)
  ½ ounce Avuá Amburana cachaça
  ¾ ounce lemon juice
  ¾ ounce Macchu Pisco
  ¾ ounce Bols genever
  1 ounce Green Tea Yogurt Syrup (page 232)
  Lime zest, for garnish

In a cocktail tin, combine all the ingredients except the garnish. Place a
2-inch ice cube in a double rocks glass. Fill the cocktail tin with 1¼-inch
ice cubes. Cover and shake vigorously. Strain the cocktail into the double
rocks glass. Garnish with lime zest.

GLASS: Double rocks   ICE: 2-inch cube   CREATORS: Leo Robitschek
and Guillermo Bravo

SCARLET KNIGHT

Cranberry and pine meet a gin sour

New Western Gin, Ramazzotti Amaro,
Rabarbaro Zucca Amaro, Douglas Fir,
Lemon, Cranberry, Mint

¼ ounce Rabarbaro Zucca amaro

½ ounce lemon juice

¾ ounce Cranberry Syrup (page 227)

¾ ounce Ramazzotti amaro

1 ounce St. George Dry Rye gin

Mint plouche, for garnish

Clear Creek Douglas Fir eau de vie,
for garnish

2 fresh cranberries, for garnish

In a cocktail tin, combine all the ingredients except the mint, eau de vie, and cranberries. Fill a cobbler glass with crushed ice. Add three 1¼-inch ice cubes to the tin, cover, and whip. Strain the cocktail into the cobbler glass. Spritz the mint plouche six times with Douglas Fir eau de vie from an atomizer. Garnish the cocktail with the fir-scented mint plouche and the cranberries.

GLASS: Cobbler   ICE: Crushed   CREATOR: Leo Robitschek

SERGEANT PEPPER

A herbaceous tequila sour with spice and green pepper

Cachaça, Highlands Blanco Tequila, Jalapeño,
Green Pepper, Pineapple, Lime, Salt

  5 drops Saline Solution (page 245)
  ¼ ounce pineapple juice
  ½ ounce lime juice
  ½ ounce Agave Syrup (page 216)
  ½ ounce Jalapeño-Infused Tequila
  (page 235)
  ¾ ounce green pepper juice
  1 ounce Avuá Prata cachaça

In a cocktail tin, combine all the ingredients. Fill the tin with 1¼-inch
ice cubes. Cover and shake. Strain the cocktail into a chilled coupe.

GLASS: Coupe   ICE: None   CREATOR: Nathan O'Neill

SHIRLEY HEIGHTS

A rum punch with bittered orange, strawberry, and almond

Antiguan Rum, Aperol, Fino Sherry, Orgeat, Passionfruit,
Strawberry, Vanilla, Lime, Mint

2 medium strawberries, 1 for muddling and 1 for garnish

1 teaspoon Passionfruit Syrup (page 240)

¼ ounce Vanilla Syrup (page 249)

½ ounce Orgeat (page 239)

½ ounce lime juice

¾ ounce Aperol

1 ounce Lustau Jarana fino sherry

1 ounce English Harbour rum

Mint plouche, for garnish

In a cocktail tin, muddle a strawberry, then add the remaining ingredients
except the garnishes. Fill a Belgium glass with crushed ice. Add three
1¼-inch ice cubes to the cocktail tin. Cover and whip vigorously. Strain
the cocktail into the Belgium glass using a hawthorne strainer and top
with additional crushed ice. Garnish with the mint plouche and remaining
strawberry.

GLASS: Belgium   ICE: Crushed   CREATOR: Julian Reingold

SOUTH PARK SLING

A bitter variation on a gin sling

London Dry Gin, Cynar, Aperol, Cherry Heering, Passionfruit, Pineapple, Lime, Coffee-Infused Angostura Bitters

4 dashes Coffee-Infused Angostura Bitters (page 225)
1 teaspoon Passionfruit syrup (page 240)
½ ounce Cherry Heering
¾ ounce lime juice
¾ ounce pineapple juice
¾ ounce Aperol
¾ ounce Cynar
¾ ounce Beefeater gin
1 ounce Seagram's club soda
Orange half-wheel, for garnish
3 mint sprigs, for garnish

In a cocktail tin, combine all the ingredients except the club soda and garnishes. Fill a highball glass with 1¼-inch ice cubes. Fill the cocktail tin with 1¼-inch ice cubes. Cover and shake vigorously. Add the club soda to the cocktail tin. Strain the cocktail into the highball glass. Skewer the orange half-wheel through the ends, place the mint sprigs through the center, and garnish the cocktail.

GLASS: Highball   ICE: 1¼-inch cubes   CREATOR: Leo Robitschek

SUMMER JAMZ

A tart berry cobbler with floral tones

———

Aquavit, Elderflower Liqueur, Rabarbaro, Lingonberry, Lemon

1 barspoon lingonberry jam
¼ ounce Rabarbaro Zucca amaro
¼ ounce St-Germain
½ ounce Cane Syrup (page 218)
¾ ounce lemon juice
1½ ounces Krogstad aquavit
2 lemon wheels, for garnish
1 raspberry, for garnish

In a cocktail tin, combine all the ingredients except the garnishes. Fill a double rocks glass with crushed ice. Cut the lemon wheels in half and skewer them in a fan shape. Add the raspberry to the top of the skewer. Add three 1¼-inch ice cubes to the cocktail tin. Cover and whip. Strain the cocktail into the double rocks glass, add additional crushed ice, and dome the top of the cocktail using a julep strainer. Garnish with the lemon wheel–raspberry fan.

GLASS: Double rocks   ICE: Crushed   CREATOR: Nathan O'Neil

THIRD PEDAL

A bergamot tequila sour with olive oil

———

Highland Blanco Tequila, Fino Sherry, Italicus, Salers, Green Tea, Sheep's Milk Yogurt, Grapefruit, Lime, Olive Oil

Grapefruit twist, for shaking
½ ounce Agave Syrup (page 216)
½ ounce lime juice
½ ounce grapefruit juice
½ ounce Salers Gentiane
½ ounce Italicus
1 ounce Green Tea Yogurt Syrup (page 232)
1 ounce Lustau Jarana fino sherry
1 ounce Olive Oil–Washed Tequila (page 239)
3 drops extra-virgin olive oil, for garnish

In a cocktail tin, combine all the ingredients except the garnish. Place a 2-inch ice cube in a double rocks glass. Fill the cocktail tin with 1¼-inch ice cubes. Cover and shake vigorously. Strain the cocktail into the double rocks glass. Garnish with the olive oil.

GLASS: Double rocks   ICE: 2-inch cube   CREATOR: Pietro Collina

TIT FOR TAT

A bitter fruit-and-caraway sour

Aquavit, Fino Sherry, Elderflower Liqueur, Yellow Chartreuse,
Raspberry, Lemon

¼ ounce yellow Chartreuse
½ ounce Raspberry Syrup (page 242)
½ ounce lemon juice
½ ounce St-Germain
1 ounce Lustau Jarana fino sherry
1 ounce Krogstad aquavit
2 raspberries, for garnish
Lemon wheel, for garnish

In a cocktail tin, combine all the ingredients except the garnishes. Fill
a double rocks glass with crushed ice. Skewer the raspberries through
the lemon wheel. Add three 1¼-inch ice cubes to the cocktail tin. Cover
and whip. Strain the cocktail into the double rocks glass, add additional
crushed ice, and dome the top of the cocktail using a julep strainer.
Garnish with the lemon wheel–raspberry flag.

GLASS: Double rocks   ICE: Crushed   CREATOR: Pietro Collina

VASA

A coconut vodka sour with caraway and fennel

Vodka, Fino Sherry, Elderflower Liqueur, Coconut, Aquavit, Absinthe, Celery, Fennel, Lemon

  1 pinch fennel seeds, for muddling
  ½-inch piece celery, for muddling
  2 dashes Pernod Absinthe
  ¼ ounce Krogstad aquavit
  Scant ½ ounce Cane Syrup (page 218)
  ½ ounce Lustau Jarana fino sherry
  ½ ounce St-Germain
  ½ ounce lemon juice
  1½ ounces Coconut-Infused Absolut Elyx (page 224)

In a cocktail tin, muddle the fennel seeds and celery, then add the remaining ingredients. Place a 2-inch ice cube in a double rocks glass. Fill the cocktail tin with 1¼-inch ice cubes. Cover and shake vigorously. Strain the cocktail into the double rocks glass.

GLASS: Double rocks   ICE: 2-inch cube   CREATOR: Julia Reingold

V.O.C.

A gingersnap cookie meets a genever sour

Genever, New Western Gin, Maple Syrup, Ginger, Cinnamon, Lemon

  1 teaspoon Cassia Cinnamon Syrup (page 218)
  ¼ ounce Spicy Ginger Syrup (page 247)
  Scant ½ ounce Grade A maple syrup
  ½ ounce St. George Dry Rye gin
  ¾ ounce lemon juice
  1½ ounces Bols genever

Combine all the ingredients in a cocktail tin. Fill the tin with ice, cover, and shake. Strain the cocktail into a coupe.

GLASS: Coupe   ICE: None   CREATOR: Jim Betz

WALTER GIBSON

A take on a savory Gibson, inspired by chenin blanc

Vodka, New American Gin, London Dry Gin, Chambery Dry
and Blanc Vermouth, Apple Brandy, Chenin Blanc, Pickle

SERVES 2

    1 teaspoon Pineapple Gomme (page 240)
    ¼ ounce St. George unaged apple brandy
    ½ ounce Moulin Touchais chenin blanc 1994
    ½ ounce Dolin de Chambery Blanc vermouth
    ½ ounce Dolin de Chambery Dry vermouth
    ½ ounce Old Raj Blue Navy Strength gin
    1 ounce Edinburgh Seaside gin
    1 ounce Absolut Elyx vodka
    6 pickled pearl onions, for garnish

In a mixing glass, combine all the ingredients except the garnish. Fill the
mixing glass with 1¼-inch ice cubes and stir. Strain the cocktail into two
Nick and Nora glasses using a hawthorne strainer. Garnish each with
3 pearl onions.

GLASS: Nick and Nora   ICE: None   CREATOR: Pietro Collina

WHEY TO GO

A lactic Collins with a touch of bitterness

———

Guyanese Rum, Cocchi Americano, Salers, Whey, White Balsamic Vinegar, Lemon, Absinthe

  2 dashes Pernod Absinthe
  7 dashes white balsamic vinegar
  ½ ounce lemon juice
  ½ ounce Salers Gentiane
  1 ounce Cocchi Americano
  1 ounce Whey Syrup (page 249)
  1 ounce El Dorado 3-Year rum
  1½ ounces Seagram's club soda
  1 dill frond, for garnish

In a cocktail tin, combine all the ingredients except the club soda and garnish. Fill a highball glass with 1¼-inch ice cubes. Fill the cocktail tin with 1¼-inch ice cubes. Cover and shake. Add the club soda to the cocktail tin. Strain the cocktail into the highball glass. Garnish with the dill frond.

GLASS: Highball   ICE: 1¼-inch cubes   CREATOR: Nathan O'Neill

DARK
SPIRITED

1903

A Manhattan variation with notes of apple and grapefruit

Apple Brandy, Cognac, Vermouth di Torino, Cocchi Americano, Grapefruit Bitters

2 dashes Scrappy's Grapefruit bitters
¾ ounce Cocchi Vermouth di Torino
¾ ounce Cocchi Americano
1 ounce Pierre Ferrand 1840 Cognac
1 ounce Laird's apple brandy

Combine all the ingredients in a mixing glass. Fill the mixing glass with ice and stir. Strain the cocktail into a coupe.

GLASS: Coupe   ICE: None   CREATOR: Jessica Gonzalez

BAUDOUINE

A tequila Manhattan with mole flavors

Añejo Highlands Tequila, Amaro Nonino, Sweet Vermouth, Cream Sherry, Crème de Cacao, Mole Bitters, Orange Bitters

1 dash House Orange Bitters (page 234)
3 dashes Bittermens Xocolatl Mole bitters
1 teaspoon Marie Brizard crème de cacao white
½ ounce Lustau East India Solera cream sherry
¾ ounce Carpano Antica Formula sweet vermouth
¾ ounce Amaro Nonino Quintessentia
1½ ounces Siete Leguas añejo tequila

Combine all the ingredients in a mixing glass. Add a 2-inch ice cube to a double rocks glass. Fill the mixing glass with ice and stir. Strain the cocktail into the double rocks glass.

GLASS: Double rocks   ICE: 2-inch cube   CREATOR: Gino Pellarin

BEAU FOUR

A springtime Manhattan with mentholated complexity and depth

Bourbon, Chambery Dry Vermouth,
Nardini Amaro, Amaro Ciociaro, Cucumber

2 whole-length cucumber slices,
1 for stirring and 1 for garnish
Scant ½ ounce Foro Amaro
½ ounce Nardini amaro
¾ ounce Dolin de Chambery Dry vermouth
1½ ounces Jim Beam Black bourbon

Combine all the ingredients except the cucumber garnish in a mixing glass. Fill the mixing glass with ice and stir. Strain the cocktail into a coupe. Skewer the remaining cucumber slice into a wave and garnish the cocktail.

GLASS: Coupe   ICE: None   CREATOR: Leo Robitschek

BEE LAVENDER

A Scotch sour with hints of lavender and honey

Blended Scotch, Cocchi Americano, Lavender-Infused Honey, Lemon

¾ ounce Lavender-Infused Honey Syrup (page 237)
¾ ounce lemon juice
¾ ounce Cocchi Americano
1½ ounces J&B blended Scotch whisky

Combine all the ingredients in a cocktail tin. Place a 2-inch ice cube in a double rocks glass. Fill the tin with ice, cover, and shake. Strain the cocktail into the double rocks glass.

GLASS: Double rocks   ICE: 2-inch cube   CREATOR: Leo Robitschek

BIRCH TREE

A cognac Manhattan reminiscent of root beer flavors

———

Cognac, Aged Aquavit, Vermouth di Torino,
Amaro Nonino, Coffee, Sarsaparilla

   2 dashes Sarsaparilla Tincture (page 245)

   ½ ounce Cold Brew Coffee Concentrate
   (page 226)

   ½ ounce Amaro Nonino

   ¾ ounce Cocchi Vermouth di Torino

   ¾ ounce Linie aquavit

   1 ounce Pierre Ferrand 1840 Cognac

   Brandied Cherry (see page 217), for garnish

   Grapefruit twist, for expressing

Combine all the ingredients except the cherry and grapefruit twist in a
mixing glass. Fill the mixing glass with ice and stir. Strain the cocktail
into a Nick and Nora glass and garnish with the brandied cherry. Express
the oils from the grapefruit twist over the cocktail, then discard the twist.

GLASS: Nick and Nora   ICE: None   CREATOR: Leo Robitschek

BITCHES BREW

A bitter-chocolate-and-coffee-tinged Manhattan

———

Rye Whiskey, Zwack Unicum, Coffee, Mole Bitters

   4 dashes Bitter Truth Xocolatl Mole bitters

   Scant ½ ounce Demerara Simple Syrup (page 227)

   ½ ounce Cold Brew Coffee Concentrate (page 226)

   ½ ounce Zwack Unicum

   2 ounces Old Overholt rye whiskey

In a chilled mixing glass, combine all the ingredients. Fill the mixing glass
with 1¼-inch ice cubes and stir. Strain the cocktail into a chilled coupe.

GLASS: Coupe   ICE: None   CREATOR: Leo Robitschek

BLACKTAIL

A Scotch sour with banana, yuzu, and almond

Islay Scotch, Jamaican Rum, Banana Liqueur, Orgeat, Lemon, Yuzu, Absinthe

2 dashes yuzu juice
3 dashes Vieux Pontarlier absinthe verte
¼ ounce Diplomático Reserva Exclusiva rum
½ ounce Orgeat (page 239)
½ ounce lemon juice
½ ounce Giffard banana liqueur
½ ounce Hamilton Jamaican gold rum
1 ounce Bowmore 12-Year Scotch

In a cocktail tin, combine all the ingredients. Place a 2-inch ice cube in a double rocks glass. Fill the cocktail tin with 1¼-inch ice cubes. Cover and shake vigorously. Strain the cocktail into the double rocks glass.

GLASS: Double rocks   ICE: 2-inch cube   CREATOR: Nicholas Rolin

BLISTERED IN THE SUN

A rye-based tiki drink with red pepper and passionfruit

Rye Whiskey, Amontillado Sherry, Red Pepper, Passionfruit, Lemon, Salt

5 drops Saline Solution (page 245)
2 dashes Angostura bitters
¼ ounce Passionfruit Syrup (page 240)
½ ounce lemon juice
¾ ounce Red Pepper Agave Syrup (page 243)
¾ ounce Lustau Los Arcos amontillado sherry
1 ounce Old Overholt rye whiskey

In a cocktail tin, combine all the ingredients. Fill a Pilsner glass with crushed ice. Add three 1¼-inch ice cubes to the cocktail tin. Cover and whip. Strain the cocktail into the Pilsner glass and top with additional crushed ice.

GLASS: Pilsner   ICE: Crushed   CREATOR: Leo Robitschek

BROADWAY

A bitter Manhattan variation named after the famous street where NoMad NYC is located

Rye Whiskey, Vermouth di Torino, Bonal, Cynar, Maraschino Liqueur, Orange and Angostura Bitters

1 dash Angostura bitters
1 dash House Orange Bitters (page 234)
1 teaspoon Luxardo Maraschino liqueur
Scant ½ ounce Cynar
½ ounce Bonal
¾ ounce Cocchi Vermouth di Torino
1 ounce Rittenhouse bonded rye whiskey
3 maraschino cherries, for garnish

In a chilled mixing glass, combine all the ingredients except the garnish. Place a 2-inch ice cube in a double rocks glass. Fill the mixing glass with 1¼-inch ice cubes and stir. Strain the cocktail into the double rocks glass. Skewer the cherries and place in the drink.

GLASS: Double rocks   ICE: 2-inch cube   CREATOR: Nathan O'Neill

BROWN SUGAR

A rum Manhattan with flavors of caramelized sugar

Aged Venezuelan Rum, Rye Whiskey, Cynar, Cream Sherry, Mole Bitters

2 dashes Bittermens Xocolatl Mole bitters
¾ ounce Lustau East India Solera cream sherry
¾ ounce Cynar
¾ ounce Rittenhouse bonded rye whiskey
1 ounce Diplomático Reserva Exclusiva rum

Combine all the ingredients in a mixing glass. Fill the mixing glass with ice and stir. Strain the cocktail into a coupe.

GLASS: Coupe   ICE: None   CREATOR: Leo Robitschek

THE BRUNSWICK

A complex, dark bitter Manhattan

Bourbon, Sweet Vermouth, Campari, Amaro Averna, Maraschino Liqueur, Angostura Bitters, Sarsaparilla

1 dash Sarsaparilla Tincture (page 245)

3 dashes Angostura bitters

1 teaspoon Luxardo Maraschino liqueur

½ ounce Amaro Averna

½ ounce Campari

½ ounce Carpano Antica Formula sweet vermouth

1½ ounces Old Grand-Dad 114 bourbon

Lemon twist, for expressing

Combine all the ingredients except the lemon twist in a mixing glass. Fill the mixing glass with ice and stir. Strain the cocktail into a coupe. Express the oils from the lemon twist over the cocktail, then discard the twist.

GLASS: Coupe   ICE: None   CREATOR: Jonathan Armstrong

CAFÉ CON LECHE

A rum-and-aquavit sour with the flavors of a cappuccino

Guayanese Rum, Aged Aquavit,
Creole Shrubb, Coffee, Orgeat,
Lemon, Egg White

   ½ ounce Cold Brew Coffee
   Concentrate (page 226)
   ½ ounce Rhum Clément Créole Shrubb
   ¾ ounce Orgeat (page 239)
   ¾ ounce lemon juice
   1 ounce Linie aquavit
   1 ounce El Dorado 15-Year rum
   1 egg white

Combine all the ingredients except the egg white in a cocktail tin, then add the egg white to the tin. Cover and dry shake to emulsify the egg white. Fill the tin with ice, cover again, and shake. Strain the cocktail into a coupe.

GLASS: Coupe   ICE: None   CREATOR: Leo Robitschek

CAMEO

A fall variation on a Sazerac

Apple Brandy, Cocchi Americano, Vermouth di Torino, Pear Eau De Vie, Yellow Chartreuse, Aged Cachaça, Apple

¼ ounce Avuá Amburana cachaça
¼ ounce yellow Chartreuse
½ ounce Clear Creek pear brandy
½ ounce Cocchi Vermouth di Torino
¾ ounce Cocchi Americano
1 ounce Laird's 7½-Year apple brandy
3 slices apple, for garnish

In a chilled mixing glass, combine all the ingredients except the garnish. Fill the mixing glass with 1¼-inch ice cubes and stir. Strain the cocktail into a single rocks glass. Skewer the apple slices into a fan shape and place on the rim of the glass.

GLASS: Single rocks   ICE: None   CREATOR: Pietro Collina

CHARLIE WATTS

A modern tiki drink with black pepper and apricot

Aged Rhum Agricole, Batavia Arrack, Guyanese Rum, Tellicherry Black Pepper, Apricot, Pineapple, Lemon

¼ ounce Lemon Hart 151 Demerara rum

¼ ounce Batavia Arrack van Oosten

½ ounce lemon juice

¾ ounce Tellicherry Black Pepper Syrup (page 248)

¾ ounce pineapple juice

¾ ounce apricot juice

1½ ounces Rhum J.M Gold rum

½ ounce Seagram's club soda, to finish

Ground black pepper, for garnish

Pineapple frond, for garnish

Combine all the ingredients except the club soda and garnishes in a cocktail tin. Fill a double rocks glass with 1¼-inch ice cubes. Fill the tin with ice, cover, and shake. Strain the cocktail into the double rocks glass and add the club soda. Garnish with a sprinkle of black pepper and a pineapple frond.

GLASS: Double rocks   ICE: 1¼-inch cubes   CREATORS: Jessica Gonzalez and Leo Robitschek

CIAMPINO

A herbaceous, spiked hotel chocolate

Fernet-Branca, Green Chartreuse, Hot Chocolate, Angostura Cream

¼ ounce Simple Syrup
(page 245), for Angostura
cream garnish

¼ ounce Angostura bitters,
for Angostura cream garnish

1 ounce cream, for Angostura
cream garnish

½ ounce green Chartreuse

¾ ounce Fernet-Branca

5 ounces Hot Chocolate Base
(page 234)

Combine the simple syrup, Angostura bitters, and cream in a cocktail tin, cover, and shake until the cream thickens but is still loose enough to pour. Fill a hot-cocktail glass with hot water in order to heat it. Combine the remaining ingredients in a small saucepan and warm over medium heat until the cocktail comes to a simmer. Discard the hot water in the cocktail glass, then pour in the cocktail. Float with the Angostura cream.

GLASS: Hot-cocktail   ICE: None   CREATOR: Leo Robitschek

CROOKED KILT

A Scotch cobbler with bittered, green pineapple notes
———

Blended Scotch, Islay Scotch, Green Chartreuse, Velvet Falernum, Lime, Pineapple

½ ounce pineapple juice
½ ounce John D. Taylor's Velvet Falernum
½ ounce green Chartreuse
¾ ounce lime juice
1½ ounces J&B blended Scotch whisky
Mint plouche, for garnish
Laphroaig 10-Year Islay Scotch, for garnish

Combine all the ingredients except the garnishes in a cocktail tin. Fill a cobbler glass with crushed ice. Add three 1¼-inch cubes to the tin, cover, and whip. Strain the cocktail into the cobbler glass. Spritz the mint plouche six times with Laphroaig from an atomizer and garnish the cocktail.

GLASS: Cobbler   ICE: Crushed   CREATOR: Leo Robitschek

DARK HORSE

A rum-and-cognac Manhattan with bitter orange and coffee
———

Cognac, Guatemalan Rum, Averna, Orange Curaçao, Coffee

½ ounce Cold Brew Coffee Concentrate (page 226)
½ ounce Grand Marnier
¾ ounce Ron Zacapa 23 rum
¾ ounce Amaro Averna
1 ounce Pierre Ferrand Ambre Cognac
Orange twist, for expressing

In a chilled mixing glass, combine all the ingredients except the orange twist. Fill the glass with 1¼-inch ice cubes and stir. Strain the cocktail into a coupe. Use a lit match to warm both sides of the orange twist, holding the match and twist close to the edge of the coupe, with the match between the peel and glass. Quickly express the orange oils from the peel so that they ignite over the drink, then discard the twist.

GLASS: Coupe   ICE: None   CREATOR: Daniel Dirth

DETOX-RETOX

A silky Old-Fashioned with hints of coconut

Blended Scotch, Venezuelan Rum, Pineapple Rum, Aged Cachaça, Coconut Water, Angostura Bitters

6 dashes Angostura bitters
1 teaspoon Avuá Amburana cachaça
¼ ounce Demerara Simple Syrup (page 227)
½ ounce Plantation pineapple rum
1 ounce Diplomático Reserva Exclusiva rum
1 ounce Chivas 12-Year Scotch
1½ ounces Harmless Harvest coconut water or fresh coconut water (do not used pasteurized)

In a double rocks glass, combine all the ingredients. Add a 2-inch ice cube and stir for 5 seconds.

GLASS: Double rocks   ICE: 2-inch cube   CREATOR: Leo Robitschek

DOS GARDENIAS PARA TI

A honey-and-nut dominant, rich tiki drink

Blended Scotch, Palo Cortado Sherry, Walnut, Maple,
Lemon, Chocolate Bitters

4 dashes Bitter Truth chocolate bitters
1 teaspoon Nux Alpina walnut liqueur
Scant ½ ounce Grade A maple syrup
½ ounce lemon juice
½ ounce Chivas 12-Year Scotch
¾ ounce Gardenia Syrup (page 230)
1½ ounces Lustau Peninsula palo cortado sherry

In a cocktail tin, combine all the ingredients. Fill a Pilsner glass with
crushed ice. Add three 1¼-inch ice cubes to the cocktail tin. Cover and
whip. Strain the cocktail into the Pilsner glass and top with additional
crushed ice.

GLASS: Pilsner   ICE: Crushed   CREATOR: Pietro Collina

DOYERS STREET

A bitter-orange Manhattan

Rye Whiskey, Chambery Dry Vermouth, China China, Elderflower Liqueur,
Angostura Bitters

2 dashes Angostura bitters
¼ ounce St-Germain
½ ounce Bigallet China China amer liqueur
¾ ounce Dolin de Chambery Dry vermouth
1½ ounces Rittenhouse bonded rye whiskey

Combine all the ingredients in a mixing glass. Place a 2-inch ice cube
in a double rocks glass. Fill the mixing glass with ice and stir. Strain the
cocktail into the double rocks glass over the 2-inch cube.

GLASS: Double rocks   ICE: 2-inch cube   CREATOR: Leo Robitschek

DR. KANANGA

A nutty and rich mai tai variation

Venezuelan Rum, Jamaican Rum, Cream Sherry,
Falernum, Orgeat, Cinnamon, Brown Butter,
Walnut Bitters, Coffee-Infused Angostura Bitters

    2 dashes Fee Brothers black walnut bitters
    1 teaspoon Ceylon Cinnamon Syrup (page 219)
    ¼ ounce Lustau East India Solera cream sherry
    ½ ounce Brown Butter Falernum (page 218)
    ½ ounce Hamilton Jamaican gold rum
    ¾ ounce Orgeat (page 239)
    ¾ ounce lemon juice
    1 ounce Diplomático Mantuano rum
    6 dashes Coffee-Infused Angostura Bitters
    (page 225), for garnish
    Mint plouche, for garnish
    Lemon wheel, for garnish
    Cinnamon stick, for garnish

In a cocktail tin, combine all the ingredients except the garnishes. Fill a
Belgium glass with crushed ice. Add three 1¼-inch ice cubes to the cocktail
tin. Cover and whip vigorously. Strain the cocktail into the Belgium glass
using a hawthorne strainer, then top with the coffee-infused Angostura
bitters and additional crushed ice. Garnish with the mint plouche, lemon
wheel, and cinnamon stick.

GLASS: Belgium   ICE: Crushed   CREATOR: Shaun Dunn

EL TIGRE

A tropical flip with the flavor of mole

Highlands Reposado Tequila, Aged Aquavit, Mole Bitters, Egg,
Ceylon Cinnamon, Lemon, Cane Sugar

1 whole egg
4 dashes Bittermens Xocolatl Mole bitters
¼ ounce Cane Syrup (page 218)
Scant ¾ ounce Ceylon Cinnamon Syrup (page 219)
¾ ounce lemon juice
1 ounce Linie aquavit
1 ounce Siete Leguas reposado tequila
1 ounce Seagram's club soda

Combine all the ingredients except the club soda in a cocktail tin. Cover
the tin and dry shake to emulsify the egg. Then fill the tin with ice, cover,
and shake again. Prime a fizz glass with the club soda. Strain the cocktail
into the fizz glass.

GLASS: Fizz   ICE: None   CREATOR: Lacy Hawkins

EN MAISON

A Japanese whisky Old-Fashioned with coffee, maple, and salt

———

Japanese Whisky, Rye Whiskey, Amontillado Sherry, Maple Syrup, Verjus, Coffee-Infused Angostura Bitters, Sea Salt

3 dashes Coffee-Infused Angostura Bitters (page 225)

1 teaspoon Fusion verjus blanc juice

Scant ½ ounce Grade A maple syrup

½ ounce Rittenhouse bonded rye whiskey

¾ ounce Lustau Los Arcos amontillado sherry

1 ounce Toki Japanese whisky

Pinch of Maldon sea salt, for garnish

In a chilled mixing glass, combine all the ingredients except the garnish. Place a 2-inch ice cube in a double rocks glass. Fill the mixing glass with 1¼-inch ice cubes and stir. Strain the cocktail into the double rocks glass. Garnish with the sea salt on top of the ice cube.

GLASS: Double rocks   ICE: 2-inch cube   CREATOR: Shaun Dunn

FIVE FAMILIES FRANK

An Italian-style Manhattan, as smooth as Frank in his suit

———

Rye Whiskey, Barolo Chinato, Amaro Averna, Rabarbaro Zucca Amaro, Maraschino Liqueur

1 teaspoon Luxardo Maraschino liqueur

¼ ounce Rabarbaro Zucca amaro

¼ ounce Amaro Averna

½ ounce Cocchi Barolo Chinato

2 ounces Rittenhouse bonded rye whiskey

Combine all the ingredients in a mixing glass. Fill the mixing glass with ice and stir. Strain the cocktail into a coupe.

GLASS: Coupe   ICE: None   CREATOR: Jonathan Armstrong

FORTUNE TELLER

A bitter rum Manhattan

———

Aged Venezuelan Rums, Bonal, Cynar

½ ounce Cynar
½ ounce Bonal
1 ounce Santa Teresa 1796 rum
1 ounce Diplomático Reserva Exclusiva rum

Combine all the ingredients in a mixing glass. Place a 2-inch ice cube in a double rocks glass. Fill the mixing glass with ice and stir. Strain the cocktail into the double rocks glass over the 2-inch cube.

GLASS: Double rocks   ICE: 2-inch cube   CREATOR: Leo Robitschek

FORTY THIEVES

A whiskey sour with bitter fruit notes

———

Rye Whiskey, Amaro Nonino, Amaro Ciociaro, Angostura Bitters, Ginger, Pineapple, Lemon

1 dash Angostura bitters
½ ounce Ginger Lime Syrup (page 231)
½ ounce lemon juice
¾ ounce pineapple juice
½ ounce Amaro Ciociaro
½ ounce Amaro Nonino Quintessentia
1 ounce Rittenhouse bonded rye whiskey

Combine all the ingredients in a cocktail tin. Place a 2-inch ice cube in a double rocks glass. Fill the tin with ice, cover, and shake. Strain the cocktail into the double rocks glass.

GLASS: Double rocks   ICE: 2-inch cube   CREATOR: Gino Pellarin

FOXTROT

A rye mai tai with tropical fruit

Bourbon, Rye Whiskey, Velvet Falernum, Orgeat, Passionfruit, Vanilla, Lime, Angostura Bitters

7 dashes Angostura bitters
¼ ounce Vanilla Syrup (page 249)
¼ ounce John D. Taylor's Velvet Falernum
¼ ounce Passionfruit Syrup (page 240)
¾ ounce Orgeat (page 239)
¾ ounce lime juice
1 ounce Rittenhouse bonded rye whiskey
1 ounce Old Forester 100 bourbon
6 dashes Coffee-Infused Angostura Bitters (page 225), for garnish
Mint plouche, for garnish
Grated nutmeg, for garnish

In a cocktail tin, combine all the ingredients except the garnishes. Fill a Pilsner glass with crushed ice. Add three 1¼-inch ice cubes to the cocktail tin. Cover and whip. Strain the cocktail into the Pilsner glass, then top with the coffee-infused Angostura bitters and additional crushed ice. Garnish with the mint plouche and grated nutmeg.

GLASS: Pilsner   ICE: Crushed   CREATOR: Leo Robitschek

GENTLEMEN'S EXCHANGE

A Manhattan variation with notes of coffee and chocolate

Rye Whiskey, Suze, Foro Amaro, Vermouth di Torino, Coffee, Absinthe, Angostura Bitters

2 dashes Angostura bitters

4 dashes Pernod Absinthe

1 teaspoon Cold Brew Coffee Concentrate (page 226)

½ ounce Foro Amaro

½ ounce Suze

¾ ounce Cocchi Vermouth di Torino

1½ ounces Rittenhouse bonded rye whiskey

Grapefruit twist, for expressing

Combine all the ingredients except the grapefruit twist in a mixing glass. Place a 2-inch ice cube in a double rocks glass. Fill the mixing glass with ice and stir. Strain the cocktail into the double rocks glass. Express the oils from the grapefruit twist over the cocktail, and discard the twist.

GLASS: Double rocks   ICE: 2-inch cube   CREATOR: Leo Robitschek

GIMME A BEET

An earthy whiskey sour with strawberries

Rye Whiskey, Aged Aquavit, Chambery Dry Vermouth, Beet, Strawberry, Jalapeño, Vanilla

    1 medium strawberry, for muddling
    1 teaspoon Vanilla Syrup (page 249)
    ¼ ounce beet juice
    ½ ounce Jalapeño-Infused Agave Syrup (page 235)
    ½ ounce Dolin de Chambery Dry vermouth
    ¾ ounce lemon juice
    ¾ ounce Linie aquavit
    ¾ ounce Rittenhouse bonded rye whiskey

In a cocktail tin, muddle the strawberry, then add all the remaining ingredients. Place a 2-inch ice cube in a double rocks glass. Fill the cocktail tin with 1¼-inch ice cubes. Cover and shake vigorously. Strain the cocktail into the double rocks glass.

GLASS: Double rocks   ICE: 2-inch cube   CREATOR: Leo Robitschek

HAIR TRIGGER

A bitter, minty, and complex dark and stormy

Aged Venezuelan Rum, Fernet-Branca,
Angostura Bitters, Ginger, Lime,
Cucumber, Mint

2 long cucumber slices, 1 for shaking
and 1 for garnish

Scant ½ ounce Angostura bitters

½ ounce Ginger Lime Syrup
(page 231)

¾ ounce Spicy Ginger Syrup
(page 247)

¾ ounce lime juice

¾ ounce Fernet-Branca

¾ ounce Pampero Aniversario rum

Mint plouche, for garnish

Combine all the ingredients except the cucumber garnish and the mint
plouche in a cocktail tin. Fill a cobbler glass with crushed ice. Add three
1¼-inch ice cubes to the tin, cover, and whip. Strain the cocktail into the
cobbler glass and top with additional crushed ice. Garnish with the mint
plouche and the remaining cucumber slice.

GLASS: Cobbler   ICE: Crushed   CREATOR: Jessica Gonzalez

JIVE TURKEY

A lighter-style Manhattan with a hint of floralness

Rye Whiskey, Bourbon, Chambery Dry Vermouth,
Amaro Ciociaro, Elderflower Liqueur, Angostura Bitters

1 dash Angostura bitters
¼ ounce St-Germain
¾ ounce Amaro Ciociaro
¾ ounce Dolin de Chambery Dry vermouth
¾ ounce Buffalo Trace bourbon
1 ounce Wild Turkey 101 whiskey
Lemon twist, for expressing

Combine all the ingredients except the lemon twist in a mixing glass.
Fill the mixing glass with ice and stir. Strain the cocktail into a coupe.
Express the oils from the lemon twist over the cocktail, then discard
the twist.

GLASS: Coupe   ICE: None   CREATOR: Jessica Gonzalez

KING'S ARMS

A caraway-and-cacao Sazerac variation

Rye Whiskey, Aged Aquavit, Amaro Averna, Crème de Cacao, Coffee

¼ ounce Cold Brew Coffee Concentrate (page 226)
¼ ounce De Kuyper crème de cacao white
¾ ounce Amaro Averna
1 ounce Linie aquavit
1 ounce Old Overholt rye whiskey

Combine all the ingredients in a mixing glass. Fill the glass with
1¼-inch ice cubes and stir. Strain the cocktail into a single rocks glass.

GLASS: Single rocks   ICE: None   CREATOR: Pietro Collina

KINGSMAN

A cereal-malt Old-Fashioned with banana

Aged Genever, Rye Whiskey, Agricole Rhum, Oloroso Sherry, Falernum, Brown Butter, Banana Liqueur

1 teaspoon Giffard banana liqueur
¼ ounce Rhum J.M Blanc Agricole Martinique 100 Proof rum
½ ounce Brown Butter Falernum (page 218)
½ ounce Lustau Don Nuño Oloroso sherry
½ ounce Woodford Reserve rye whiskey
1 ounce Old Duff single malt genever

Combine all the ingredients in a mixing glass. Place a 2-inch ice cube in a double rocks glass. Fill the mixing glass with ice and stir. Strain the cocktail into the double rocks glass.

GLASS: Double rocks   ICE: 2-inch cube   CREATOR: Nathan O'Neill

LITTLE DRAGON

A complex Old-Fashioned with salted plums and dark chocolate

———

Cacao Nib–Infused Cognac, Pineau des Charentes, Genever, Aged Aquavit, Plum Vinegar, Umeboshi

  1 teaspoon Demerara Simple Syrup (page 227)
  ¼ ounce Taiwanese plum vinegar
  ½ ounce Linie aquavit
  ½ ounce Bols genever
  ¾ ounce Paul-Marie & Fils Pineau des Charentes
  ¾ ounce Cacao Nib–Infused Pierre Ferrand 1840 Cognac (page 223)
  Umeboshi paste, for garnish

In a mixing glass, combine all the ingredients except the garnish. Using a brush, paint a brushstroke of umeboshi paste in a double rocks glass, starting at the inside bottom and going straight up to the top, then paint from the top of the glass one-third of the way down the front, following the same line you created on the inside. Place a 2-inch ice cube in the double rocks glass. Fill the mixing glass with 1¼-inch ice cubes and stir. Strain the cocktail into the double rocks glass using a hawthorne strainer.

GLASS: Double rocks   ICE: 2-inch cube   CREATOR: Leo Robitschek

LITTLE RED ROOSTER

A fruit-forward whiskey sour

Irish Whiskey, Barolo Chinato, Strega, Aperol, Thai Bird Chile,
Strawberry, Lemon

Small strawberry, for muddling
½ ounce Thai Bird Chile–Infused Aperol (page 249)
½ ounce Strega
¾ ounce lemon juice
1 ounce Cocchi Barolo Chinato
1 ounce Jameson Irish whiskey

Muddle the strawberry in a cocktail tin and then add the remaining
ingredients. Fill the tin with ice, cover, and shake. Strain the cocktail
into a coupe.

GLASS: Coupe   ICE: None   CREATORS: Leo Robitschek
                                              and Jessica Gonzalez

MADAME LAVEAU

A herbaceous rum Manhattan

Aged Guyanese Rum, Aged Aquavit, Amontillado Sherry, Pale Cream Sherry, Strega, Angostura Bitters, Absinthe

1 dash Angostura bitters
¼ ounce Strega
½ ounce Alvear Pale cream sherry
½ ounce Lustau Los Arcos amontillado sherry
¾ ounce Linie aquavit
¾ ounce El Dorado 15-Year rum
Pernod Absinthe, as a rinse
Orange twist, for garnish

Combine all the ingredients except the absinthe and orange twist in a mixing glass. Rinse a coupe glass with six sprays of absinthe from an atomizer. Fill the mixing glass with ice and stir. Strain the cocktail into the rinsed coupe. Flame the orange twist over the drink and place it skin side up in the glass.

GLASS: Coupe   ICE: None   CREATOR: Jim Kearns

MADISON PARK SMASH

A richer-style smash named after Madison Park

Cognac, Royal Combier, Angostura Bitters,
Lemon, Demerara, Mint

¼ ounce Demerara Simple
Syrup (page 227)

¾ ounce lemon juice

1 ounce Royal Combier

1 ounce Jean Grosperrin
VSOP Cognac

5 mint leaves

Mint plouche, for garnish

6 dashes Angostura bitters,
for garnish

Combine the demerara syrup, lemon juice, Royal Combier, and Cognac
in a cocktail tin. Clap the mint leaves between your hands to release their
oils, then drop them in the tin. Fill a double rocks glass with crushed ice.
Add three 1¼-inch ice cubes to the tin, cover, and gently whip to chill
and aerate the cocktail without overly bruising the mint leaves. Strain
the cocktail into the double rocks glass. Fill the glass with more crushed
ice and make a mound of crushed ice up over the rim of the glass. Insert
straws and the mint plouche beside the mound, just inside the glass.
Decorate the ice dome with the Angostura bitters.

GLASS: Double rocks   ICE: Crushed   CREATOR: Leo Robitschek

MANHATTAN MILK PUNCH

A clarified milk punch with flavors of a tropical Manhattan cocktail

Rye Whiskey, Venezuelan Rum, Sweet Vermouth, Foro Amaro, Squash, Clarified Milk, Pineapple, Lemon, Spices

SERVES 3

   3 ounces whole milk
   1 ounce lemon juice
   1 ounce Kabocha Squash Syrup (page 236)
   1 ounce Foro Amaro
   1 ounce Rittenhouse bonded rye whiskey
   1 ounce Diplomático Reserva Exclusiva rum
   1½ ounces pineapple juice
   1½ ounces Dolin de Chambery Rouge vermouth

In a small saucepan, warm the milk over medium heat, stirring continuously, until it starts steaming. Make sure that it doesn't boil or burn. Remove from the heat and add the lemon juice. Give the mixture a quick stir; it should start curdling. In a large container, combine the curdled milk with all the remaining ingredients. Hang a superbag over an empty container. If you don't have a superbag, get a large toddy filter and hang it over the large container, or cover a chinois with a few layers of cheesecloth. Pour the liquid into the superbag, when the liquid that is coming out starts running clear you should have a layer of milk curds in the superbag. Make sure you do not break this layer, as it's the clarification layer of the punch. Allow the remaining liquid to drip through and clarify. For each serving, place a 2-inch ice cube in a double rocks glass and pour in about 4 ounces of the milk punch.

GLASS: Double rocks   ICE: 2-inch cube   CREATOR: Leo Robitschek

MASS A-PEELLE

A delicate, light, fragrant cobbler with savory squash notes, named after Billy Peelle

Venezuelan Rum, Amontillado Sherry, Squash, Lemon,
Spices, Angostura Bitters

- 2 dashes Angostura bitters
- 1 teaspoon Cane Syrup (page 218)
- ½ ounce Kabocha Squash Syrup (page 236)
- ½ ounce lemon juice
- ½ ounce Diplomático Reserva Exclusiva rum
- 1½ ounces Lustau Los Arcos amontillado sherry
- Lemon wheel, for garnish

Combine all the ingredients except the lemon wheel in a cocktail tin.
Fill a highball glass with crushed ice. Add three 1¼-inch ice cubes to the
tin, cover, and whip vigorously. Strain the cocktail into the highball glass.
Top with additional crushed ice to reach the rim of the glass. Insert the
lemon wheel along the back of the glass. Mound with additional crushed
ice so that it rests against the citrus wheel high above the rim of the glass.

GLASS: Highball   ICE: Crushed   CREATOR: Leo Robitschek

MATCHLOCK

A high-proof whiskey zombie variation

Bourbon, Rye Whiskey, Angostura Bitters, Absinthe,
Ginger, Vanilla Syrup, Grenadine, Lemon, Grapefruit

    2 dashes Pernod Absinthe
    3 dashes Angostura bitters
    ¼ ounce Grenadine (page 232)
    ¼ ounce Ginger Lime Syrup (page 231)
    ½ ounce Spicy Ginger Syrup (page 247)
    ½ ounce Vanilla Syrup (page 249)
    ¾ ounce lemon juice
    ¾ ounce grapefruit juice
    1 ounce Old Overholt rye whiskey
    1 ounce Rittenhouse bonded rye whiskey
    1 ounce Knob Creek Single Barrel Reserve bourbon
    Mint plouche, for garnish

Combine all the ingredients except the mint in a cocktail tin. Fill a snifter
with crushed ice. Add three 1¼-inch ice cubes to the tin, cover, and whip.
Strain the cocktail into the snifter and top with additional crushed ice.
Garnish with the mint plouche.

GLASS: Snifter   ICE: Crushed   CREATOR: Jonathan
                                                       Armstrong

MILES AHEAD

A herbaceous whiskey sour with cardamom

Rye Whiskey, Aged Aquavit, Chambery Blanc Vermouth, Amontillado Sherry, Velvet Falernum, Lemon, Honey, Cardamom, Orange Bitters

- 2 cardamom pods, for muddling
- 2 dashes House Orange Bitters (page 234)
- ¼ ounce Honey Syrup (page 233)
- ½ ounce John D. Taylor's Velvet Falernum
- ½ ounce Lustau Los Arcos amontillado sherry
- ½ ounce Dolin de Chambery Blanc vermouth
- ½ ounce lemon juice
- ¾ ounce Linie aquavit
- ¾ ounce Rittenhouse bonded rye whiskey

In a cocktail tin, lightly muddle the cardamom pods, then add the remaining ingredients. Fill the tin with 1¼-inch ice cubes. Cover and shake vigorously. Strain the cocktail into a chilled coupe.

GLASS: Coupe   ICE: None   CREATOR: Pietro Collina

MOTT AND MULBERRY

A whiskey sour that tastes like mulled cider

———

Rye Whiskey, Amaro Abano, Honeycrisp Apple, Lemon, Demerara

Scant ½ ounce lemon juice

½ ounce Demerara Simple Syrup (page 227)

¾ ounce Honeycrisp apple cider

¾ ounce Luxardo Amaro Abano

1 ounce Old Overholt rye whiskey

3 slices red apple, for garnish

Combine all the ingredients except the garnish in a cocktail tin. Fill a double rocks glass with 1¼-inch ice cubes. Fill the tin with ice, cover, and shake. Strain the cocktail into the double rocks glass. Skewer the apple slices into a fan shape and place on the rim of the glass.

GLASS: Double rocks   ICE: 1¼-inch cubes   CREATOR: Leo Robitschek

MYNAH BIRD

A stirred tiki drink with the flavors of a Jungle Bird cocktail

———

Guyanese Rum, Blackstrap Rum, Sweet Vermouth, Campari, Crème de Cacao, Mole Bitters

5 dashes Bittermens Xocolatl Mole bitters

1 teaspoon De Kuyper crème de cacao

¼ ounce Cruzan Black Strap rum

½ ounce Campari

¾ ounce Carpano Antica Formula sweet vermouth

1 ounce El Dorado 15-Year rum

In a chilled mixing glass, combine all the ingredients. Place a 2-inch ice cube in a double rocks glass. Fill the mixing glass with 1¼-inch ice cubes and stir. Strain the cocktail into the double rocks glass.

GLASS: Double rocks   ICE: 2-inch cube   CREATOR: Nathan O'Neill

NORTH SEA OIL

A spirit-forward cocktail with smoke, bitter orange,
chocolate, and caraway ... doesn't quite fit any box

———

Aged Aquavit, Cocchi Americano,
Islay Scotch, Triple Sec

¼ ounce Combier triple sec

½ ounce Laphroaig 10-Year Islay
Scotch

¾ ounce Cocchi Americano

1½ ounces Linie aquavit

Grapefruit twist, for garnish

Combine all the ingredients except the grapefruit twist in a mixing glass.
Place a 2-inch cube in a double rocks glass. Fill the mixing glass with ice
and stir. Strain the cocktail into the double rocks glass over the 2-inch
cube. Express the oils from the grapefruit twist over the cocktail, and
place it in the drink.

GLASS: Double rocks   ICE: 2-inch cube   CREATOR: Leo Robitschek

OLD ALHAMBRA

A rich Scotch Manhattan with smoke and cacao

———

Islay Scotch, Chambery Blanc Vermouth, Cream Sherry, Crème de Cacao

½ ounce Marie Brizard crème de cacao white

½ ounce Lustau East India Solera cream sherry

¾ ounce Dolin de Chambery Blanc vermouth

1½ ounces Laphroaig 10-Year Islay Scotch

Grapefruit twist, for garnish

Combine all the ingredients except the grapefruit twist in a mixing glass.
Fill the mixing glass with ice and stir. Strain the cocktail into a coupe.
Express the oils from the grapefruit twist over the cocktail, and place
it in the drink.

GLASS: Coupe   ICE: None   CREATOR: Leo Robitschek

ORIGINAL SIN

A fig-forward, rich brandy sour with hints of young coconut

Brandy de Jerez, Fig Leaf, Honey, Lemon, Aromatic Bitters

4 dashes Bitter Truth aromatic bitters
1 teaspoon Honey Syrup (page 233)
Scant ½ ounce lemon juice
½ ounce Fig Leaf Syrup (page 230)
Heavy 1½ ounces Lustau Brandy de Jerez Solera Reserva

In a cocktail tin, combine all the ingredients. Place a 2-inch ice cube in a double rocks glass. Fill the cocktail tin with 1¼-inch ice cubes. Cover and shake vigorously. Strain the cocktail into the double rocks glass.

GLASS: Double rocks   ICE: 2-inch cube   CREATOR: Pietro Collina

PANDAN EXPRESS

A complex, coconutty, and easy-drinking Scotch sour with layers of flavor

Blended Scotch, Aged Cachaça, Pale Cream Sherry, Falernum, Brown Butter, Pandan, Orgeat, Lemon, Coconut Water

1 barspoon Hamilton pimento dram
¼ ounce Tuaca
½ ounce Brown Butter Falernum (page 218)
½ ounce Orgeat (page 239)
½ ounce lemon juice
½ ounce Avuá Amburana cachaça
½ ounce Alvear Pale cream sherry
¾ ounce Harmless Harvest coconut water or fresh coconut water (do not used pasteurized)
1 ounce Pandan-Infused Johnnie Walker Black Label Scotch (page 240)

In a cocktail tin, combine all the ingredients. Place a 2-inch ice cube in a double rocks glass. Fill the cocktail tin with 1¼-inch ice cubes. Cover and shake vigorously. Strain the cocktail into the double rocks glass.

GLASS: Double rocks   ICE: 2-inch cube   CREATOR: Nathan O'Neill

PICO AND ROBINSON

A drink inspired by Leo's grandmother's Passover macaroons, with hints of coffee

Bourbon, Yellow Chartreuse, Punt e Mes, Chambery Blanc Vermouth, Coconut, Coffee, Sea Salt

    5 drops Saline Solution (page 245)
    1 teaspoon Cold Brew Coffee Concentrate (page 226)
    ½ ounce Dolin de Chambery Blanc vermouth
    ¾ ounce Carpano Punt e Mes vermouth
    ¾ ounce Yellow Chartreuse
    ¾ ounce Coconut-Infused Michter's Bourbon (page 224)
    Pinch of Maldon sea salt, for garnish

In a chilled mixing glass, combine all the ingredients except the garnish. Place a 2-inch ice cube in a double rocks glass. Fill the mixing glass with 1¼-inch ice cubes and stir. Strain the cocktail into the double rocks glass. Garnish with the sea salt on top of the ice cube.

GLASS: Double rocks   ICE: 2-inch cube   CREATOR: Leo Robitschek

PURPLE DRAGON

An earthy whiskey piña colada

Rye Whiskey, Bourbon, Angostura Bitters, Dragon Carrots, Coconut, Pineapple, Absinthe

2 dashes Pernod Absinthe

½ ounce pineapple juice

¾ ounce purple dragon carrot juice

¾ ounce Coconut Syrup (page 225)

¾ ounce Angostura bitters

¾ ounce Rittenhouse bonded rye whiskey

¾ ounce Old Forester 100 bourbon

Cinnamon stick, for garnish

3 pineapple fronds, for garnish

Lime zest, for garnish

Combine all the ingredients except the garnishes in a cocktail tin. Fill a Pilsner glass with crushed ice. Add three 1¼-inch ice cubes to the cocktail tin, cover, and whip. Strain the cocktail into the Pilsner glass and top with additional crushed ice. Briefly light the top of a cinnamon stick until it smokes and place it into the drink for garnish. Garnish with the pineapple fronds and lime zest.

GLASS: Pilsner   ICE: Crushed   CREATOR: Leo Robitschek

REPOSSESSION

A tequila sour with stone fruit and smoke

Highlands Tequila, Amontillado Sherry, Apricot Liqueur,
Mezcal, Lemon, Cane Sugar

¼ ounce Cane Syrup (page 218)
½ ounce lemon juice
½ ounce Rothman & Winter apricot liqueur
¾ ounce Lustau Los Arcos amontillado sherry
1 ounce Don Julio reposado tequila
Sombra mezcal, to finish

Combine all the ingredients except the mezcal in a cocktail tin. Place a
2-inch ice cube in a double rocks glass. Fill the cocktail tin with ice, cover,
and shake. Strain the cocktail into the double rocks glass. Spritz the surface
of the cocktail six times with Sombra mezcal from an atomizer.

GLASS: Double rocks   ICE: 2-inch cube   CREATOR: Leo Robitschek

RINGO

A lightly spiced whiskey sour with caraway, apple, and cucumber

Japanese Rice Whiskey, Aged Aquavit, Rye Whiskey, Apple, Mustard, Cucumber, Absinthe

1 cucumber slice

2 dashes Vieux Pontarlier absinthe

1 teaspoon dell'Erborista amaro

¼ ounce John D. Taylor's Velvet Falernum

½ ounce Agave Syrup (page 216)

½ ounce Wild Turkey 101 rye whiskey

½ ounce O.P. Anderson aquavit

½ ounce lime juice

¾ ounce green apple juice

¾ ounce Mustard Seed-Infused Kikori Whiskey (page 238)

In a cocktail tin, combine all the ingredients. Place a 2-inch ice cube in a double rocks glass. Fill the cocktail tin with 1¼-inch ice cubes. Cover and shake vigorously. Strain the cocktail into the double rocks glass.

GLASS: Double rocks   ICE: 2-inch cube   CREATOR: Joey Smith

RIPTIDE

An anise-forward mai tai variation

Batavia Arrack, Jamaican Rum, Green Chartreuse, Maraschino Liqueur,
Orgeat, Passionfruit, Pineapple, Lime, Absinthe

2 dashes Pernod Absinthe
1 teaspoon Luxardo Maraschino liqueur
¼ ounce Passionfruit Syrup (page 240)
½ ounce Orgeat (page 239)
½ ounce lime juice
½ ounce pineapple juice
½ ounce green Chartreuse
¾ ounce Hamilton Jamaican gold rum
¾ ounce Batavia Arrack van Oosten
6 dashes Coffee-Infused Angostura Bitters (page 225), for garnish
Mint plouche, for garnish
Cucumber slice, for garnish

In a cocktail tin, combine all the ingredients except the garnishes. Fill a
snifter with crushed ice. Add three 1¼-inch ice cubes to the cocktail tin.
Cover and whip. Strain the cocktail into the snifter glass, then top with
the coffee-infused Angostura bitters and additional crushed ice. Garnish
with the mint plouche and cucumber slice.

GLASS: Snifter   ICE: Crushed   CREATOR: Jack Schramm

ROCK AND A HARD PLACE

A nutty Manhattan

———

Rye Whiskey, Chambery Dry Vermouth, Sweet Vermouth,
Amaro Nonino, Walnut

2 dashes Fee Brothers black walnut bitters

1 teaspoon Nux Alpina walnut liqueur

½ ounce Amaro Nonino Quintessentia

½ ounce Carpano Antica Formula sweet vermouth

½ ounce Dolin de Chambery Dry vermouth

1½ ounces Rittenhouse bonded rye whiskey

Combine all the ingredients in a mixing glass. Fill the mixing glass with
ice and stir. Strain the cocktail into a Nick and Nora glass.

GLASS: Nick and Nora   ICE: None   CREATOR: Alisa Bobcat Robovsky

THE ROOTS

An earthy kitchen-centric mai tai with chocolate

———

Aged Aquavit, Chambery Blanc Vermouth, Cocchi Americano, Celery Root, Chamomile, White Balsamic Vinegar, Chocolate Bitters

   6-inch celery stalk, for garnish

   2 dashes Bitter Truth chocolate bitters

   10 dashes white balsamic vinegar

   1 barspoon Chamomile Honey Syrup (page 221)

   ¾ ounce Cocchi Americano

   ¾ ounce Celery Root–Infused Dolin de Chambery
   Blanc Vermouth (page 219)

   1 ounce Linie aquavit

Using a vegetable peeler, shave a strip from the celery stalk, starting at the top of the stalk and pulling down until you reach the bottom, creating a celery curl. Roll the curl tightly and place in ice water. In a chilled mixing glass, combine the remaining ingredients. Place a 2-inch ice cube in a double rocks glass. Fill the mixing glass with 1¼-inch ice cubes and stir. Strain the cocktail into the double rocks glass. Garnish with the celery curl on top of the ice cube.

GLASS: Double rocks   ICE: 2-inch cube   CREATOR: Leo Robitschek

SATAN'S CIRCUS

A rye whiskey sour with chile, cherry, and bitter orange

Rye Whiskey, Thai Bird Chile, Aperol,
Barolo Chinato, Lemon

   ¾ ounce lemon juice
   ¾ ounce Barolo Chinato
   ¾ ounce Thai Bird Chile–Infused Aperol
   (page 249)
   2 ounces Old Overholt rye whiskey

Combine all the ingredients in a cocktail tin.
Fill the tin with ice, cover, and shake. Strain the
cocktail into a coupe.

GLASS: Coupe   ICE: None   CREATOR: Leo Robitschek

SCOTCH DUMPLING

An apple brandy sour with aromatic pepper

Apple Brandy, Islay Scotch, Amaro Montenegro, Black Pepper,
Lemon, Egg White

   ¾ ounce Tellicherry Black Pepper Syrup (page 248)
   ¾ ounce lemon juice
   ¾ ounce Amaro Montenegro
   ¾ ounce Laphroaig 10-Year Islay Scotch
   1 ounce Laird's apple brandy
   1 egg white

Combine all the ingredients except the egg white in a cocktail tin, then
add the egg white to the tin. Cover the tin and dry shake to emulsify
the egg white. Fill the tin with ice, cover again, and shake. Strain the
cocktail into a coupe.

GLASS: Coupe   ICE: None   CREATOR: Josh Shweesti
                                          Ben-Yaish

SMOKING JACKET

A Manhattan variation with smoked tea

Bourbon, Marseilles Dry Vermouth, Crème de Cacao, Triple Sec, Campari, Lapsang Souchong Tea

¼ ounce Campari

¼ ounce Combier triple sec

½ ounce Lapsang Souchong–Infused
De Kuyper Crème de Cacao (page 236)

¾ ounce Noilly Prat Original Dry vermouth

1 ounce Buffalo Trace bourbon

In a mixing glass, combine all the ingredients. Fill the mixing glass with 1¼-inch ice cubes and stir. Strain the cocktail into a Nick and Nora glass using a hawthorne strainer.

GLASS: Nick and Nora   ICE: None   CREATOR: Shaun Dunn

SONS OF LIBERTY

A fall sour with apple and Earl Grey

Bourbon, Apple Brandy, Amaro Abano,
Earl Grey, Lemon, Egg White

¼ ounce Luxardo Amaro Abano
¾ ounce lemon juice
¾ ounce Earl Grey Syrup (page 228)
1 ounce Laird's apple brandy
1 ounce Jim Beam Black bourbon
1 egg white
Ground Tellicherry black pepper, for garnish

Combine all the ingredients except the egg white and black pepper in a
cocktail tin, then add the egg white to the tin. Cover the tin and dry shake
to emulsify the egg white. Fill the tin with ice, cover again, and shake.
Strain the cocktail into a coupe. When the egg white settles, add a pinch
of Tellicherry pepper to the top of the cocktail in a half-moon shape.
Swirl the coupe a few times to stretch the half-moon into a spiral.

GLASS: Coupe   ICE: None   CREATOR: Leo Robitschek

SPICED CARROT COLADA (COLD)

A carrot cake–flavored piña colada

———

Angostura Bitters, Blackstrap Rum,
Foro Amaro, Coconut, Carrots, Pineapple

    1 barspoon Cane Syrup (page 218)
    ½ ounce pineapple juice
    ½ ounce Foro Amaro
    ½ ounce Cruzan Black Strap rum
    ¾ ounce carrot juice
    1 ounce Coconut Syrup (page 225)
    1 ounce Angostura bitters
    3 pineapple fronds, for garnish

Combine all the ingredients except the pineapple fronds in a cocktail tin. Fill a Pilsner glass with crushed ice. Add three 1¼-inch ice cubes to the cocktail tin, cover, and whip. Strain the cocktail into the Pilsner glass and top with additional crushed ice. Garnish with the pineapple fronds.

GLASS: Pilsner   ICE: Crushed   CREATOR: Leo Robitschek

SPICED CARROT COLADA (HOT)

A warm carrot cake–flavored piña colada

———

Angostura Bitters, Blackstrap Rum, Foro Amaro, Coconut, Carrots, Pineapple

½ ounce pineapple juice

½ ounce Foro Amaro

½ ounce Cruzan Black Strap rum

¾ ounce carrot juice

1 ounce water

1 ounce Coconut Syrup (page 225)

1 ounce Angostura bitters

Fill a hot-cocktail glass with hot water in order to heat it. Combine all the ingredients in a small saucepan and warm over medium heat until the cocktail comes to a simmer. Discard the hot water in the cocktail glass, then pour in the cocktail.

GLASS: Hot-cocktail   ICE: None   CREATOR: Leo Robitschek

SPRING STING

A stirred savory grasshopper

———

Cognac, Cocchi Americano, Islay Scotch, Chareau, Nardini Amaro, Cucumber

1 teaspoon Nardini amaro

½ ounce Chareau

½ ounce Laphroaig 10-Year Scotch

¾ ounce Cocchi Americano

1 ounce Pierre Ferrand 1840 Cognac

¼ cucumber

In a mixing glass, combine all the ingredients except the cucumber. Using a melon baller, cut a dime-size ball out of the cucumber. Fill the mixing glass with 1¼-inch ice cubes and stir. Strain the cocktail into a Nick and Nora glass using a hawthorne strainer. Skewer the cucumber ball and garnish the cocktail.

GLASS: Nick and Nora   ICE: None   CREATOR: Pietro Collina

START ME UP

A whiskey sour with honey and ginger

———

**Bourbon, Trinidadian Rum, Strega,
Orange Bitters, Honey, Ginger, Lemon**

4 dashes House Orange Bitters
(page 234)

¼ ounce Spicy Ginger Syrup
(page 247)

¼ ounce Honey Syrup (page 233)

½ ounce Strega

½ ounce Scarlet Ibis rum

¾ ounce lemon juice

1 ounce Elijah Craig 12-Year bourbon

Combine all the ingredients in a cocktail tin. Place a 2-inch ice cube in a double rocks glass. Fill the tin with ice cubes, cover, and shake. Strain the cocktail into the double rocks glass.

GLASS: Double rocks   ICE: 2-inch cube   CREATORS: Leo Robitschek
and Jessica Gonzalez

TAXI DANCER

A spicy whiskey sour with red wine

———

**Bonded Rye Whiskey, Bourbon, Thai Bird Chile, Aperol, Strega,
Barolo Chinato, Lemon**

¼ ounce Simple Syrup (page 245)

½ ounce Strega

½ ounce Cocchi Barolo Chinato

½ ounce Elijah Craig 12-Year bourbon

¾ ounce lemon juice

¾ ounce Thai Bird Chile–Infused Aperol (page 249)

¾ ounce Rittenhouse bonded rye whiskey

Combine all the ingredients in a cocktail tin. Fill the tin with ice cubes, cover, and shake. Strain the cocktail into a coupe.

GLASS: Coupe   ICE: None   CREATOR: Leo Robitschek

THICK AS THIEVES

A rum Old-Fashioned with banana and cacao

Guyanese Rum, Irish Whiskey, Amontillado and Cream Sherry, Crème de Cacao, Banana Liqueur, Maple Syrup, Absinthe, Chocolate Bitters

2 dashes Bitter Truth chocolate bitters

3 dashes Pernod Absinthe

1 teaspoon Grade A maple syrup

1 teaspoon Giffard banana liqueur

¼ ounce De Kuyper crème de cacao

¼ ounce Lustau East India Solera cream sherry

¼ ounce Lustau Los Arcos amontillado sherry

½ ounce Connemara Irish whiskey

¾ ounce Jameson Black Barrel Irish whiskey

¾ ounce El Dorado 15-Year rum

In a chilled mixing glass, combine all the ingredients. Place a 2-inch ice cube in a double rocks glass. Fill the mixing glass with 1¼-inch ice cubes and stir. Strain the cocktail into the double rocks glass.

GLASS: Double rocks   ICE: 2-inch cube   CREATOR: Alex Lerman

TINSELTOWN REBELLION

An agricole rum punch with passionfruit and melon

Haitian Rhum, Jamaican Rum, Aged Cachaça,
Allspice Dram, Yogurt, Passionfruit

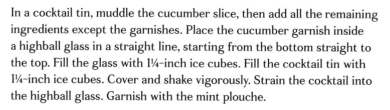

Cucumber slice, for muddling, plus whole-length
cucumber slice, for garnish

1 teaspoon St. Elizabeth allspice dram

¼ ounce Passionfruit Syrup (page 240)

¼ ounce Smith & Cross Navy Strength Jamaican rum

Scant ½ ounce lime juice

½ ounce Tellicherry Black Pepper Syrup (page 248)

½ ounce Avuá Amburana cachaça

1 ounce Green Tea Yogurt Syrup (page 232)

1 ounce Santa Claus melon juice

1 ounce Boukman rhum

Mint plouche, for garnish

In a cocktail tin, muddle the cucumber slice, then add all the remaining
ingredients except the garnishes. Place the cucumber garnish inside
a highball glass in a straight line, starting from the bottom straight to
the top. Fill the glass with 1¼-inch ice cubes. Fill the cocktail tin with
1¼-inch ice cubes. Cover and shake vigorously. Strain the cocktail into
the highball glass. Garnish with the mint plouche.

GLASS: Highball   ICE: 1¼-inch cubes   CREATOR: Tyler Caffall

TIVOLI

A stirred celery-añejo Old-Fashioned; savory with a touch of acidity

Añejo Tequila, Amaro Nonino, Unicum Plum, Cocchi Americano, Palo Cortado Sherry, White Balsamic Vinegar, Celery

6-inch celery stalk, for garnish, plus 1-inch celery stalk, for muddling

7 dashes white balsamic vinegar

½ ounce Lustau Peninsula palo cortado sherry

½ ounce Zwack Unicum Plum

½ ounce Siembra Azul añejo tequila

¾ ounce Cocchi Americano

1 ounce Amaro Nonino Quintessentia

Using a vegetable peeler, shave a strip from the 6-inch celery stalk, starting at the top of the stalk and pulling down until you reach the bottom, creating a celery curl. Roll the curl tightly and place in ice water. In a chilled mixing glass, lightly muddle the 1-inch celery piece, then add all the remaining ingredients except the garnish. Place a 2-inch ice cube in a double rocks glass. Fill the mixing glass with 1¼-inch ice cubes and stir. Strain the cocktail into the double rocks glass. Garnish with the celery curl on top of the ice cube.

GLASS: Double rocks   ICE: 2-inch cube   CREATOR: Nathan O'Neill

TOPANGA

A tequila tiki cocktail with chai and yogurt

Añejo Tequila, Aged Cachaça, Chai, Yogurt, Turmeric, Lemon, Angostura Bitters

2 dashes Angostura bitters
½ ounce Agave Syrup (page 216)
Scant ¾ ounce lemon juice
1 ounce Chai-Turmeric Yogurt Syrup (page 220)
1 ounce Avuá Amburana cachaça
1 ounce Siete Leguas añejo tequila
Lime zest, for garnish

In a cocktail tin, combine all the ingredients except the garnish. Fill a Pilsner glass with crushed ice. Add three 1¼-inch ice cubes to the cocktail tin. Cover and whip. Strain the cocktail into the Pilsner glass and top with additional crushed ice. Garnish with lime zest.

GLASS: Pilsner   ICE: Crushed   CREATOR: David Bonatesta

VAGABOND

A smoky Scotch Old-Fashioned with hints of anise

Islay Scotch, Rye Whiskey, Bonal, Amontillado Sherry,
Pedro Ximénez Sherry, Absinthe

Scant ½ ounce Lustau San Emilio Pedro Ximénez sherry
½ ounce Lustau Los Arcos amontillado sherry
½ ounce Bonal
¾ ounce Rittenhouse bonded rye whiskey
1 ounce Laphroaig 10-Year Islay Scotch
Pernod Absinthe, as a rinse
Lemon twist, for expressing

Combine all the ingredients except the absinthe and lemon twist in a
mixing glass. Rinse a single rocks glass with six sprays of absinthe from
an atomizer. Fill the mixing glass with ice and stir. Strain the cocktail
into the single rocks glass. Express the oils from the lemon twist over
the cocktail, then discard the twist.

GLASS: Single rocks   ICE: None   CREATOR: Leo Robitschek

WHEELER AND WILSON

A floral, springtime Manhattan

Bourbon, Aged Venezuelan Rum, Amontillado Sherry,
Chambery Blanc Vermouth, Amaro Montenegro

2 whole-length cucumber slices, 1 for mixing and 1 for garnish
½ ounce Amaro Montenegro
½ ounce Dolin de Chambery Blanc vermouth
½ ounce Lustau Los Arcos amontillado sherry
¾ ounce Diplomático Reserva Exclusiva rum
1 ounce Old Forester 100 bourbon

Combine all the ingredients except the cucumber garnish in a mixing glass. Fill the mixing glass with ice and stir. Strain the cocktail into a coupe. Skewer the remaining cucumber slice into a wave shape and garnish the drink.

GLASS: Coupe   ICE: None   CREATOR: Leo Robitschek

WIT THE COCO

A piña colada that is herbaceous and spirituous

Aged Aquavit, Green Chartreuse, Velvet Falernum, Coconut, Lime, Pineapple

¼ ounce John D. Taylor's Velvet Falernum

½ ounce green Chartreuse

½ ounce Coconut Syrup (page 225)

½ ounce lime juice

¾ ounce pineapple juice

¾ ounce Linie aquavit

6 dashes Angostura bitters, for garnish

2 pineapple fronds, for garnish

In a cocktail tin, combine all the ingredients except the garnishes. Fill a highball glass with crushed ice. Add three 1¼-inch ice cubes to the cocktail tin. Cover and whip vigorously. Strain the cocktail into the highball glass. Add the Angostura bitters and top with additional crushed ice. Garnish with the pineapple fronds.

GLASS: Highball   ICE: Crushed   CREATOR: Pietro Collina

CLASSICS

ADONIS

A sherry Manhattan with fall spice

———

Chai, Vermouth di Torino, Fino and Amontillado Sherry

4 dashes House Orange Bitters (page 234)
¼ ounce Lustau East India Solera cream sherry
½ ounce Lustau Los Arcos amontillado sherry
1 ounce Lustau Jarana fino sherry
1½ ounces Chai-Infused Cocchi Vermouth di Torino (page 220)

In a chilled mixing glass, combine all the ingredients. Fill the mixing glass with 1¼-inch ice cubes and stir. Strain the cocktail into a chilled coupe.

GLASS: Coupe   ICE: None

AMARETTO SOUR

Our take on a guilty pleasure, an almond sour with a touch of bitterness

———

Amaretto, Campari, Lemon, Orange, Egg White

1 egg white
1 teaspoon Simple Syrup (page 245)
¼ ounce Campari
½ ounce orange juice
¾ ounce lemon juice
2 ounces Disaronno amaretto
3 drops Angostura bitters, for garnish

In a cocktail tin, combine all the ingredients except the garnish. Seal and dry shake to emulsify the egg white into the cocktail. Carefully open the tin and fill with 1¼-inch ice cubes. Seal it again and shake vigorously. Strain the cocktail into a chilled coupe using a hawthorne strainer and a fine tea strainer. Once the egg white settles, use a Japanese bitters dasher to carefully dot the Angostura bitters around the rim of the glass. Use a cocktail pick to connect the dots into a half-circle.

GLASS: Coupe   ICE: None

APEROL SOUR

A bitter and citrus-forward sour with hints of strawberry

Aperol, Lemon, Egg White

   1 egg white
   ½ ounce Cane Syrup (page 218)
   1 ounce lemon juice
   2 ounces Aperol
   3 drops Peychaud's bitters, for garnish

In a cocktail tin, combine all the ingredients except the garnish. Seal and dry shake to emulsify the egg white into the cocktail. Carefully open the tin and fill with 1¼-inch ice cubes. Seal it again and shake vigorously. Strain the cocktail into a chilled coupe using a hawthorne strainer and a fine tea strainer. Once the egg white settles, use a Japanese bitters dasher to carefully dot the Peychaud's bitters around the rim of the glass. Use a cocktail pick to connect the dots into a half-circle.

GLASS: Coupe   ICE: None

BADMINTON CUP

A variation on a refreshing sangria

Pinot Noir, Moscatel Sherry, Maraschino Liqueur, Lemon, Mint

2 cucumber slices, 1 for muddling and 1 for garnish
5 mint leaves, for muddling
½ ounce Cane Syrup (page 218)
½ ounce Luxardo Maraschino liqueur
½ ounce Seagram's club soda
¾ ounce lemon juice
¾ ounce Lustau Emilín Moscatel sherry
1½ ounces Pinot Noir
Mint plouche, for garnish

In a cocktail tin, muddle a cucumber slice and the mint leaves, then add the remaining ingredients except the garnishes. Fill a highball glass with crushed ice. Add three 1¼-inch ice cubes to the tin. Cover and whip. Strain the cocktail into the highball glass and top with additional crushed ice. Garnish with the mint plouche and remaining cucumber slice inserted down the side of the glass at an angle.

GLASS: Highball   ICE: Crushed

BAMBOO

A nutty, umami-forward sherry Manhattan

Amontillado Sherry, Cream Sherry, Chambery
Dry Vermouth, Angostura Bitters, Orange Bitters

2 dashes Angostura bitters
4 dashes House Orange Bitters (page 234)
¾ ounce Lustau Los Arcos amontillado sherry
1 ounce Lustau East India Solera cream sherry
1½ ounces Dolin de Chambery Dry vermouth
Lemon twist, for garnish

Combine all the ingredients except the lemon twist in a mixing glass. Fill the mixing glass with ice and stir. Strain the cocktail into a coupe.

Express the oils from the lemon twist over the glass, and insert it in the cocktail.

GLASS: Coupe ICE: None

BIJOU

A herbaceous, bitter, and rich martini

———

Plymouth Gin, Sweet Vermouth, Green Chartreuse, Orange Bitters

2 dashes House Orange Bitters (page 234)
¾ ounce green Chartreuse
1 ounce Carpano Antica Formula sweet vermouth
1½ ounces Plymouth gin
Lemon twist, for garnish

Combine all the ingredients except the lemon twist in a mixing glass. Fill the mixing glass with ice and stir. Strain the cocktail into a coupe. Express the oils from the lemon twist over the glass, and insert it in the cocktail.

GLASS: Coupe ICE: None

BIJOU RESERVE

A more refined take on a Bijou

———

Aged London Dry Gin, Sweet Vermouth, Yellow Chartreuse, Green Chartreuse

¼ ounce yellow Chartreuse V.E.P.
¼ ounce green Chartreuse V.E.P.
1 ounce Carpano Antica Formula vermouth
1½ ounces Burrough's Reserve gin

In a chilled mixing glass, combine all the ingredients. Fill the mixing glass with 1¼-inch ice cubes and stir. Strain the cocktail into a chilled coupe.

GLASS: Coupe ICE: None

BLINKER

A whiskey sour with grapefruit and raspberry

Rye Whiskey, Islay Scotch, Raspberry, Grapefruit, Lime

   ¼ ounce Cane Syrup (page 218)
   ¼ ounce Raspberry Syrup (page 242)
   ½ ounce lime juice
   1 ounce grapefruit juice
   1½ ounces George Dickel rye whiskey
   6 spritzes Laphroaig 10-Year Scotch, for garnish

In a cocktail tin, combine all the ingredients except the garnish. Fill the tin with 1¼-inch ice cubes. Cover and shake. Strain the cocktail into a chilled coupe. Garnish with the Scotch.

GLASS: Coupe   ICE: None

BLUE HAWAIIAN

A vegetal variation on a tropical 1950s classic

Guatemalan Rum, Green Chartreuse,
Bitter Orange, Coconut, Pineapple, Lime

   ¼ ounce Rhum Clément Créole Shrubb infused
   with 1 drop organic blue food coloring
   ½ ounce green Chartreuse
   ½ ounce Coconut Syrup (page 225)
   ½ ounce lime juice
   ¾ ounce pineapple juice
   ¾ ounce Ron Zacapa 23 rum
   5 dashes Angostura bitters, for garnish
   5 drops Peychaud's bitters, for garnish
   3 pineapple fronds, for garnish
   2 Brandied Cherries (page 217), for garnish

In a cocktail tin, combine all the ingredients except the garnishes. Fill a Pilsner glass with crushed ice. Add three 1¼-inch ice cubes to the cocktail tin. Cover and whip. Strain the cocktail into the Pilsner glass, add both bitters, and top with additional crushed ice. Garnish with the pineapple fronds and cherries.

GLASS: Pilsner   ICE: Crushed

BRANDY CRUSTA

A Cognac sour with hints of cherry

VSOP Cognac, Triple Sec, Maraschino Liqueur, Angostura Bitters, Lemon

   1 dash Angostura Bitters
   ¼ ounce Simple Syrup (page 245)
   ¼ ounce Luxardo Maraschino liqueur
   ½ ounce lemon juice
   ½ ounce Combier triple sec
   2 ounces Jean Grosperrin VSOP Cognac
   Lemon wedge, for rimming
   Sugar, for rimming
   Lemon peel horse's neck, for garnish

Combine all the ingredients except the lemon wedge, sugar, and lemon peel in a cocktail tin. Use the lemon wedge to moisten the rim of a Champagne flute and rim with the sugar. Fill the flute with crushed ice. Add three 1¼-inch ice cubes to the cocktail tin, cover, and whip. Strain the cocktail into the Champagne flute. Express the lemon horse's neck over the flute, then insert part of it into the flute so that it cascades down the side of the glass without falling out.

GLASS: Champagne flute   ICE: Crushed

CLOVER CLUB

A gin sour with raspberry

London Dry Gin, Raspberry, Lemon,
Peychaud's Bitters, Egg White

  1 egg white
  ¼ ounce Cane Syrup (page 218)
  ½ ounce Raspberry Syrup (page 242)
  ¾ ounce lemon juice
  2 ounces Fords gin
  Peychaud's bitters, for garnish

In a cocktail tin, combine all the ingredients except the Peychaud's
bitters. Cover and dry shake vigorously. Then fill the tin with ice, cover,
and shake again. Strain the cocktail into a coupe. Once the egg white
settles, use a Japanese bitters dasher to carefully add several drops of
Peychaud's bitters around the rim of the glass. Use a cocktail pick to
connect the dots of bitters into a half-circle.

GLASS: Coupe   ICE: None

COFFEE COCKTAIL

A classic flip that tastes like cappuccino

VSOP Cognac, Port, Demerara, Egg

  1 whole egg
  ½ ounce Demerara Simple Syrup (page 227)
  1 ounce Jean Grosperrin VSOP Cognac
  1½ ounces Taylor Fladgate 10-Year tawny port
  Nutmeg, for garnish

Combine all the ingredients except the nutmeg in a cocktail tin. Close
the tin and dry shake to emulsify the egg into the cocktail. Fill the tin with
ice, cover again, and shake vigorously. Strain the cocktail into a fizz glass.
Once the egg settles, use a Microplane to grate fresh nutmeg over the
surface of the cocktail.

GLASS: Fizz   ICE: None

CREOLE CONTENTMENT

A nutty Cognac Manhattan with cherry

————

Cognac, Islay Scotch, Marsala Wine, Foro Amaro,
Maraschino Liqueur, Orange Bitters

    1 dash House Orange Bitters (page 234)
    ¼ ounce Luxardo Maraschino liqueur
    ¼ ounce Bowmore 12-Year Scotch
    ½ ounce Foro Amaro
    1 ounce Marco De Bartoli Marsala Superiore 10-Year Riserva
    1 ounce Pierre Ferrand 1840 Cognac

In a chilled mixing glass, combine all the ingredients. Fill the mixing glass
with 1¼-inch ice cubes and stir. Strain the cocktail into a chilled Nick and
Nora glass.

GLASS: Nick and Nora   ICE: None

DAIQUIRI

A classic rum sour meant to be enjoyed quickly

————

Nicaraguan Rum, Lime, Cane Sugar

    ¾ ounce Cane Syrup (page 218)
    1 ounce lime juice
    2 ounces Flor de Caña 4-Year Extra Dry rum

In a cocktail tin, combine all the ingredients. Fill the tin with ice, cover,
and shake. Strain the cocktail into a coupe.

GLASS: Coupe   ICE: None

DEMERARA DRY FLOAT

A daiquiri variation with passionfruit and berries

Nicaraguan Rum, Maraschino Liqueur,
Passionfruit, Lime, Mint, Raspberries

SERVES 15

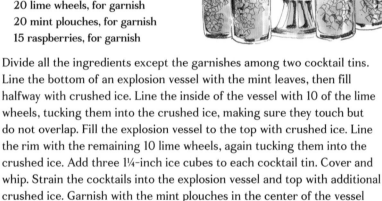

3 ounces Hamilton 151 Demerara rum

3½ ounces Luxardo Maraschino Liqueur

5¼ ounces Passionfruit Syrup (page 240)

5¼ ounces lime juice

10½ ounces Flor de Caña Rum
4-Year white

15 mint leaves, for garnish

20 lime wheels, for garnish

20 mint plouches, for garnish

15 raspberries, for garnish

Divide all the ingredients except the garnishes among two cocktail tins.
Line the bottom of an explosion vessel with the mint leaves, then fill
halfway with crushed ice. Line the inside of the vessel with 10 of the lime
wheels, tucking them into the crushed ice, making sure they touch but
do not overlap. Fill the explosion vessel to the top with crushed ice. Line
the rim with the remaining 10 lime wheels, again tucking them into the
crushed ice. Add three 1¼-inch ice cubes to each cocktail tin. Cover and
whip. Strain the cocktails into the explosion vessel and top with additional
crushed ice. Garnish with the mint plouches in the center of the vessel
and add the raspberries to the immediate left of the plouches.

GLASS: Explosion vessel   ICE: Crushed

DIPLOMAT

A low-ABV Manhattan variation made with vermouth

———

Marseilles Dry Vermouth, Ambrato Vermouth, Maraschino Liqueur, Grapefruit Bitters

Grapefruit twist for expressing

3 dashes Scrappy's Grapefruit bitters

1 teaspoon Luxardo Maraschino liqueur

1½ ounces Martini & Rossi Riserva Speciale Ambrato vermouth

1½ ounces Noilly Prat Extra Dry vermouth

In a chilled mixing glass, express the oils from the grapefruit twist, discard the twist, and then add the remaining ingredients. Fill the mixing glass with 1¼-inch ice cubes and stir. Strain the cocktail into a chilled coupe.

GLASS: Coupe   ICE: None

DON'T GIVE UP THE SHIP

A bitter and rich martini

———

London Dry Gin, Sweet Vermouth, Orange Curaçao, Fernet-Branca

1 teaspoon Fernet-Branca

¼ ounce Grand Marnier

1 ounce Carpano Antica Formula vermouth

2 ounces Tanqueray gin

Lemon twist, for garnish

In a chilled mixing glass, combine all the ingredients except the garnish. Fill the mixing glass with 1¼-inch ice cubes and stir. Strain the cocktail into a chilled coupe. Express the lemon twist over the drink and then insert it into the glass.

GLASS: Coupe   ICE: None

EGG NOG

A classic holiday nog with a kick

Venezuelan Rum, Bourbon, Blended Scotch,
Cognac, Frangelico, Egg, Cream, Nutmeg

SERVES 15

6 eggs, separated
8 ounces sugar
16 ounces cream
32 ounces milk
2 ounces Frangelico
4 ounces J&B blended Scotch whisky
6 ounces Old Forester 86 bourbon
6 ounces Pierre Ferrand 1840 Cognac
6 ounces Diplomático Reserva Exclusiva rum
1 whole nutmeg

Place the egg whites in a 5-quart bowl and the egg yolks in a separate
5-quart bowl. Add 6 ounces of the sugar to the bowl with egg yolks, then
whisk until the yolks turn pale yellow and thicken. Whisk in the cream,
followed by the milk, Frangelico, Scotch, bourbon, Cognac, and rum.
Grate the nutmeg over the top and whisk until combined.

Add the remaining 2 ounces sugar to the egg whites and whisk until stiff
peaks form. Slowly whisk into the egg yolk–spirits mixture. Reserve in an
airtight container, refrigerated, for up to 2 weeks. When ready to serve,
pour a serving into a festive mug and garnish with freshly grated nutmeg.

GLASS: Festive mug   ICE: None

EL PRESIDENTE

A rum martini with hints of fruit

Nicaraguan Rum, Chambery Blanc Vermouth, Triple Sec, Grenadine

> 1 barspoon Grenadine (page 232)
> 1 barspoon Combier triple sec
> 1½ ounces Dolin de Chambery Blanc vermouth
> 1½ ounces Caña Brava rum
> Grapefruit twist, for garnish

In a chilled mixing glass, combine all the ingredients except the garnish. Fill the mixing glass with 1¼-inch ice cubes and stir. Strain the cocktail into a chilled coupe. Express the grapefruit twist over the drink and then insert it into the glass.

GLASS: Coupe   ICE: None

FOURTH DEGREE

A richer martini with anise

London Dry Gin, Sweet Vermouth, Chambery Dry Vermouth, Absinthe

> 2 dashes Pernod Absinthe
> ½ ounce Dolin de Chambery Dry vermouth
> 1 ounce Carpano Antica Formula sweet vermouth
> 2 ounces Beefeater London dry gin
> Brandied Cherry (see page 217), for garnish

Combine all the ingredients except the cherry in a mixing glass. Place the cherry into a coupe. Fill the mixing glass with ice and stir. Strain the cocktail into the coupe.

GLASS: Coupe   ICE: None

GRASSHOPPER

A rich and creamy mint-chocolate cocktail

———

Crème de Menthe, Crème de Cacao, Fernet-Branca, Cream, Mint

  3 mint leaves, plus 1 mint sprig, for garnish
  ½ ounce Fernet-Branca
  ½ ounce De Kuyper crème de menthe
  ¾ ounce Marie Brizard crème de cacao
  1 ounce heavy cream

In a cocktail tin, combine all the ingredients except the garnish. Fill the tin with 1¼-inch ice cubes. Seal and shake. Strain the cocktail into a chilled Nick and Nora glass using a hawthorne strainer and a fine tea strainer. Garnish with the mint sprig.

GLASS: Nick and Nora   ICE: None

GREEN BEAST

An absinthe sour with cucumber

———

Absinthe, Cucumber, Lime

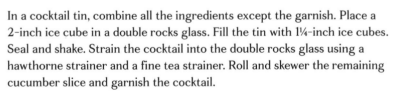

  2 cucumber slices, for shaking, plus whole-length cumber slice, for garnish
  ¾ ounce Simple Syrup (page 245)
  ¾ ounce lime juice
  1 ounce Pernod Absinthe
  1 ounce water

In a cocktail tin, combine all the ingredients except the garnish. Place a 2-inch ice cube in a double rocks glass. Fill the tin with 1¼-inch ice cubes. Seal and shake. Strain the cocktail into the double rocks glass using a hawthorne strainer and a fine tea strainer. Roll and skewer the remaining cucumber slice and garnish the cocktail.

GLASS: Double rocks   ICE: 2-inch cube

HEMINGWAY DAIQUIRI

A daiquiri variation with grapefruit bitterness

Nicaraguan Rum, Maraschino Liqueur, Grapefruit, Lime

   2 lime twists, for shaking
   ¼ ounce Cane Syrup (page 218)
   ½ ounce Luxardo Maraschino liqueur
   ½ ounce grapefruit juice
   ¾ ounce lime juice
   2 ounces Flor de Caña 4-Year Extra Dry rum

Combine all the ingredients in a cocktail tin. Fill the tin with ice, cover, and shake. Strain the cocktail into a coupe.

GLASS: Coupe   ICE: None

HONI HONI

A whiskey mai tai

Rye Whiskey, Bourbon, Marseilles Vermouth, Dry Curaçao,
Banana Liqueur, Orgeat, Lime, Coffee

   ½ ounce Giffard banana liqueur
   ½ ounce Pierre Ferrand Dry curaçao
   ½ ounce Coffee-Infused Dry Vermouth (page 226)
   ¾ ounce lime juice
   ¾ ounce George Dickel rye whiskey
   ¾ ounce Old Forester 86 bourbon
   Scant 1 ounce Orgeat (page 239)
   Banana leaf, for garnish

In a cocktail tin, combine all the ingredients except the garnish. Wrap the banana leaf on the inside of a Belgium glass and fill with crushed ice. Add three 1¼-inch ice cubes to the cocktail tin. Cover and whip vigorously. Strain the cocktail into the Belgium glass using a hawthorne strainer and top with additional crushed ice.

GLASS: Belgium   ICE: Crushed

HUNTSMAN

A funky vodka sour

Jamaican Rum, Vodka, Lemon, Angostura Bitters

2 dashes Angostura bitters
¾ ounce Simple Syrup (page 245)
¾ ounce lemon juice
1 ounce Absolut vodka
1 ounce Smith & Cross Navy Strength Jamaican rum

Combine all the ingredients in a cocktail tin. Fill the tin with ice, cover, and shake. Strain the cocktail into a coupe.

GLASS: Coupe   ICE: None

IMPROVED WHISKEY COCKTAIL

An Old-Fashioned with anise and a touch of smoke

Irish Whiskey, Islay Scotch, Blended Scotch, Maraschino Liqueur, Absinthe, Orange Bitters

3 dashes Pernod Absinthe
4 dashes House Orange Bitters (page 234)
1 teaspoon Luxardo Maraschino liqueur
¼ ounce Demerara Simple Syrup (page 227)
½ ounce Laphroaig 10-Year Islay Scotch
½ ounce Jameson Black Barrel Irish whiskey
1 ounce Bushmills Irish whiskey
Lemon twist, for garnish
Orange twist, for garnish

Combine all the ingredients except the garnishes in a mixing glass. Place a 2-inch ice cube in a double rocks glass. Fill the mixing glass with ice and stir. Strain the cocktail into the double rocks glass. Express the oils from the lemon and orange twists over the glass, and insert them in the drink.

GLASS: Double rocks   ICE: 2-inch cube

IMPROVED WHISKEY COCKTAIL RESERVE

A combination of amazing whiskies showcased at their finest

———

Japanese Whisky, Islay Scotch, Irish Whiskey, Maraschino Liqueur, Absinthe, Orange Bitters

3 dashes Pernod absinthe

4 dashes House Orange Bitters (page 234)

1 teaspoon Luxardo Maraschino liqueur

¼ ounce Demerara Simple Syrup (page 227)

½ ounce Laphroaig 10-Year Islay Scotch

¾ ounce Redbreast 15-Year Irish whiskey

¾ ounce Hibiki Harmony Japanese whisky

Lemon twist, for garnish

Orange twist, for garnish

In a mixing glass, combine all the ingredients except the garnishes. Place a 2-inch ice cube in a double rocks glass. Fill the mixing glass with 1¼-inch ice cubes and stir. Strain the cocktail into the double rocks glass. Express the oils from the lemon twist and orange twist over the glass, and insert them in the cocktail.

GLASS: Double rocks   ICE: 2-inch cube

JACK ROSE

An apple brandy sour with pomegranate

———

Calvados, Apple Brandy, Grenadine, Lemon, Lime

½ ounce lemon juice

½ ounce lime juice

¾ ounce Grenadine (page 232)

1 ounce Laird's apple brandy

1 ounce Roger Groult 3-Year Calvados Pays d'Auge

Combine all the ingredients in a cocktail tin. Fill the tin with ice, cover, and shake. Strain the cocktail into a coupe.

GLASS: Coupe   ICE: None

JUNGLE BIRD

A bitter and malty rum sour

Guyanese Rum, Blackstrap Rum, Campari,
Pineapple, Lime

½ ounce Demerara Simple Syrup (page 227)
½ ounce lime juice
¾ ounce Campari
1 ounce pineapple juice
1 ounce Cruzan Black Strap rum
1 ounce El Dorado 12-Year rum
2 pineapple fronds, for garnish

Combine all the ingredients except the pineapple fronds in a cocktail
tin. Place a 2-inch ice cube in a double rocks glass. Fill the cocktail tin
with ice. Cover and shake. Strain the cocktail into the double rocks glass.
Garnish with the pineapple fronds placed along the back of the glass.

GLASS: Double rocks   ICE: 2-inch cube

MAI TAI

A quintessential tiki cocktail with almond and citrus

———

Aged Guyanese Rum, Aged Jamaican Rum, Overproof
Agricole Rum, Orange Liqueur, Orgeat, Lime

  1 lime twist
  1 teaspoon Cane Syrup (page 218)
  ½ ounce Clément Créole Shrubb
  Liqueur d'Orange
  ½ ounce Rhum J.M Blanc Agricole Martinique
  100 Proof rum
  ¾ ounce Orgeat (page 239)
  ¾ ounce Appleton V/X Jamaican rum
  ¾ ounce El Dorado 12-Year rum
  1 ounce lime juice
  Mint plouche, for garnish

Combine all the ingredients except the mint in a cocktail tin. Fill a tiki
mug with crushed ice. Add three 1¼-inch ice cubes to the tin, cover, and
whip. Strain the cocktail into the tiki mug and top with additional crushed
ice. Garnish with the mint plouche.

GLASS: Tiki mug   ICE: Crushed

MARTINEZ

A richer, darker variant of the martini

———

Old Tom Gin, Sweet Vermouth, Angostura Bitters, Maraschino Liqueur

  2 dashes Angostura bitters
  1 teaspoon Luxardo Maraschino liqueur
  1 ounce Carpano Antica sweet vermouth
  2 ounces Hayman's Old Tom gin
  Lemon twist, for garnish

Combine all the ingredients except the lemon twist in a mixing glass. Fill the
mixing glass with ice and stir. Strain the cocktail into a coupe. Express
the oils from the lemon twist over the glass and insert it in the cocktail.

GLASS: Coupe   ICE: None

MINT JULEP

A boozy, minty, and refreshing whiskey cocktail

Bourbon, Demerara, Mint

5 mint leaves
½ ounce Demerara Simple Syrup (page 227)
2½ ounces Mint-Infused Bourbon (page 238)
Mint plouche, for garnish

Swab the inside of a frozen julep cup with the mint leaves, coating its sides with the oils. Place the leaves in a cocktail tin. Fill the julep cup with crushed ice. Add the demerara syrup and bourbon to the tin. Add three 1¼-inch ice cubes to the tin, cover, and whip. Strain the cocktail into the julep cup. Add crushed ice until it is level with the rim of the cup. Insert the plouche into the julep cup. Place two small straws into the cup. Without disturbing the mint or straws, mound crushed ice up over the rim of the cup. Be careful not to touch the frosted sides of the julep cup.

GLASS: Julep cup   ICE: Crushed

MONTAUK

A lighter Negroni variation

Navy Strength Gin, Sweet Vermouth, Chambery Blanc Vermouth, Punt e Mes, Peychaud's Bitters

6 dashes Peychaud's bitters
¼ ounce Carpano Punt e Mes vermouth
¾ ounce Dolin de Chambery Blanc vermouth
¾ ounce Carpano Antica Formula sweet vermouth
1 ounce Hayman's Royal Dock gin
Lemon twist, for garnish

In a chilled mixing glass, combine all the ingredients except the garnish. Place a 2-inch ice cube in a double rocks glass. Fill the mixing glass with 1¼-inch ice cubes and stir. Strain the cocktail into the double rocks glass. Express the lemon twist over the cocktail and place the twist into the drink.

GLASS: Double rocks   ICE: 2-inch cube

MORNING GLORY FIZZ

A whiskey sour with anise

———

Blended Scotch, Absinthe, Lemon, Egg White

   1 teaspoon Pernod Absinthe, plus as a rinse
   ¾ ounce Cane Syrup (page 218)
   ¾ ounce lemon juice
   2 ounces Chivas 12-year Scotch
   1 egg white

Combine all the ingredients except the egg white and absinthe rinse in a cocktail tin. Add the egg white to the tin, cover, and dry shake to emulsify the egg white into the cocktail. Rinse a fizz glass by spraying it six times with absinthe from an atomizer. Fill the tin with ice, cover again, and shake vigorously. Strain the cocktail into the fizz glass.

GLASS: Fizz   ICE: None

NEW YORK SOUR

A whiskey sour with mulled cider

———

Bourbon, Mulled Wine, Lemon, Egg White

   1 egg white
   ¾ ounce Simple Syrup (page 245)
   ¾ ounce lemon juice
   1¾ ounces Elijah Craig 12-Year bourbon
   ¾ ounce mulled wine, to float

In a cocktail tin, combine all the ingredients except the mulled wine. Seal and dry shake to emulsify the egg white into the cocktail. Carefully open the tin and fill with 1¼-inch ice cubes. Seal it again and shake vigorously. Strain the cocktail into a chilled coupe using a hawthorne strainer and a fine tea strainer. Once the egg white settles, float the mulled wine on top of the drink.

GLASS: Coupe   ICE: None

PALOMA

A refreshing tequila drink with grapefruit

Blanco Highlands Tequila, Mezcal,
Grapefruit, Lime, Agave, Salt

   1 lime wedge, for rimming and garnish

   Salt, for rimming

   2 ounces Seagram's club soda,
   plus more to top

   ½ ounce Agave Syrup (page 216)

   ½ ounce Sombra mezcal

   ¾ ounce lime juice

   1 ounce grapefruit juice

   1½ ounces Excellia Blanco tequila

Use the lime wedge to moisten the top inch of the outer rim of a highball
glass and rim half the glass with salt; reserve the wedge. Fill the glass
with 1¼-inch ice cubes, then prime it with the club soda. Add the agave
syrup, mezcal, lime juice, grapefruit juice, and tequila to a cocktail tin.
Add three 1¼-inch ice cubes to the tin, cover, and whip. Strain the
cocktail into the highball glass. Top the glass with additional club soda.
Garnish with the lime wedge.

GLASS: Highball   ICE: 1¼-inch cubes

PENICILLIN

A honeyed ginger Scotch sour

———

Scotch, Islay Scotch, Ginger, Honey, Lemon

¼ ounce Honey Syrup (page 233)
½ ounce Spicy Ginger Syrup (page 247)
¾ ounce lemon juice
2 ounces J&B blended Scotch whisky
¼ ounce Laphroaig 10-Year Scotch, to float

Combine all the ingredients except the Laphroaig in a cocktail tin. Place a 2-inch ice cube in a double rocks glass. Fill the tin with ice, cover, and shake. Strain the cocktail into the double rocks glass. Float the Laphroaig on top of the drink.

GLASS: Double rocks   ICE: 2-inch cube   CREATOR: Sammy Ross

PHILADELPHIA FISH HOUSE PUNCH

A rum punch with peach and ginger

———

Apple Brandy, Jamaican Rum, Crème de Pêche, Ginger, Lime, Orange Bitters

2 dashes House Orange Bitters (page 234)
¼ ounce Massenez Crème de Pêche
¼ ounce Cruzan Black Strap rum
¼ ounce Smith & Cross Navy Strength Jamaican rum
½ ounce Appleton Signature Blend rum
¾ ounce Ginger Lime Syrup (page 231)
¾ ounce lemon juice
1 ounce Laird's apple brandy
Mint plouche, for garnish

In a cocktail tin, combine all the ingredients except the garnish. Fill a highball glass with crushed ice. Add three 1¼-inch ice cubes to the cocktail tin. Cover and whip vigorously. Strain the cocktail into the highball glass and top with additional crushed ice. Garnish with the mint plouche.

GLASS: Highball   ICE: Crushed

PIMM'S CUP

A refreshing highball with ginger and a slight bitterness

Pimm's No. 1, Lime, Ginger, Orange,
Cucumber, Mint, Angostura Bitters

2 orange half-wheels, 1 for muddling
and 1 for garnish

2 cucumber slices, 1 for muddling
and 1 for garnish

¼ ounce Demerara Simple Syrup (page 227)

1 ounce Fever-Tree ginger ale

1 dash Angostura bitters

½ ounce Ginger Lime Syrup (page 231)

¾ ounce lime juice

2 ounces Pimm's No. 1 liqueur

Mint plouche, for garnish

In a cocktail tin, muddle an orange half-wheel and a cucumber slice with
the demerara syrup. Fill a highball glass with 1¼-inch ice cubes and prime
it with the ginger ale. Add the rest of the ingredients except the garnishes
to the tin and shake. Strain the cocktail into the highball glass. Garnish
with the mint plouche, a cucumber slice, and an orange half-wheel.

GLASS: Highball   ICE: 1¼-inch cubes

PIÑA COLADA

An island concoction rounded out with coconut and pineapple

———

Aged Guyanese Rum, Jamaican Rum, Rhum Agricole, Coconut, Pineapple, Heavy Cream, Angostura Bitters

¼ ounce cream
½ ounce Rhum Clément Première Canne rum
½ ounce Smith & Cross Navy Strength Jamaican rum
1 ounce Coconut Syrup (page 225)
1 ounce El Dorado 15-Year rum
1½ ounces pineapple juice
3 pineapple fronds, for garnish
1 dash Angostura bitters, for garnish

Combine all the ingredients except the pineapple fronds and bitters in a cocktail tin. Fill a Belgian glass with crushed ice. Add three 1¼-inch ice cubes to the tin, cover, and whip. Strain the cocktail into the Belgian glass and top with additional crushed ice. Garnish with the pineapple fronds, inserted in a fan shape along the back of the glass and then the bitters.

GLASS: Belgian   ICE: Crushed

PINEAPPLE DAIQUIRI

A classic daiquiri with pineapple

———

Nicaraguan Rum, Pineapple Rum, Pineapple, Lime

¾ ounce Simple Syrup (page 245)
¾ ounce lime juice
1 ounce pineapple juice
1 ounce Plantation pineapple rum
1 ounce Flor de Caña 4-Year Extra Dry rum
1 dash Angostura bitters, for garnish

Combine all the ingredients except the garnish in a cocktail tin. Fill the tin with ice, cover, and shake. Strain the cocktail into a coupe and top with the bitters.

GLASS: Coupe   ICE: None

PINEAPPLE JULEP

A refreshing gin cocktail with pineapple and berries

Old Tom Gin, Genever, Maraschino Liqueur, Charred Pineapple,
Rhubarb, Verjus, Lemon, Mint

5 mint leaves, for shaking

1 lemon twist, for shaking

6 raspberries, 3 for shaking and 3 for garnish

1 teaspoon Cane Syrup (page 218)

1 teaspoon Luxardo Maraschino liqueur

¼ ounce lemon juice

¼ ounce Rhubarb Shrub (page 243)

½ ounce Fusion verjus blanc juice

½ ounce Bols genever

1 ounce Charred Pineapple Syrup (page 221)

1 ounce Hayman's Old Tom gin

½ ounce Seagram's club soda, to float

Mint plouche, for garnish

½ slice pineapple, for garnish

Fill a julep cup with crushed ice. Place the mint leaves, lemon twist, and
3 raspberries in a cocktail tin. Add the remaining ingredients except the
club soda and garnishes. Add three 1¼-inch ice cubes to the tin. Cover and
whip vigorously. Strain the cocktail into the julep cup using a hawthorne
strainer. Float the club soda over the top and add additional crushed ice
until the ice is level with the rim of the julep cup. Holding the mint plouche
by its stem, swat it against your palm to release its aromatic oils. Insert
the plouche into the julep cup, just along its rim. Add the ½ slice pineapple
and remaining 3 raspberries next to the mint. Place two small straws into
the cup next to the mint. Pack crushed ice into a julep strainer to create a
dome shape. Without disturbing the mint or straws, flip the julep strainer
and force the ice dome down onto the julep cup to create an ice dome up
over the rim of the cup. Be careful not to touch the julep cup, so as not to
disturb its frosted sides.

GLASS: Julep cup   ICE: Crushed

SHERRY COBBLER

A low-ABV, refreshing cobbler with a nutty finish

Fino Sherry, Pedro Ximénez Sherry,
Pineapple Gomme, Lemon, Orange

2 lemon wheels, 1 for shaking
and 1 for garnish

2 orange half-wheels, 1 for shaking and
1 for garnish

½ ounce Pineapple Gomme (page 240)

3 ounces Lustau Jarana fino sherry

½ ounce Lustau San Emilio
Pedro Ximénez sherry, to finish

Combine all the ingredients except the Pedro Ximénez and garnishes in
a cocktail tin. Fill a highball glass with crushed ice. Add three 1¼-inch ice
cubes to the tin, cover, and whip vigorously, pulverizing the citrus wheels.
Strain the cocktail into the highball glass. Top with additional crushed
ice to reach the rim of the glass. Insert the remaining lemon wheel
and orange half-wheel along the back of the glass so that they are half
overlapping. Mound with additional crushed ice so that it rests against
the citrus wheels high above the rim of the glass. Finish with the Pedro
Ximénez.

GLASS: Highball   ICE: Crushed

SHERRY PAINKILLER

An easy-drinking piña colada variation with orange

————

Amontillado Sherry, Guatemalan Rum, Pineapple,
Coconut, Orange, Lime

> 2 lime wedges, plus lime juice as needed
> ½ ounce Ron Zacapa 23 rum
> ½ ounce orange juice
> 1 ounce pineapple juice
> 1 ounce Coconut Syrup (page 225)
> 2 ounces Lustau Los Arcos amontillado sherry
> Orange wheel, for garnish
> 3 pineapple fronds, for garnish

Squeeze the lime wedges into a jigger and then fill the jigger with lime
juice to get a heavy ¼ ounce. In a cocktail tin, combine the lime juice,
lime rinds, and remaining ingredients except the garnishes. Fill a snifter
with crushed ice. Add three 1¼-inch ice cubes to the cocktail tin. Cover
and whip. Strain the cocktail into the snifter and top with additional
crushed ice. Garnish with the orange wheel and pineapple fronds.

GLASS: Snifter   ICE: Crushed

TURF COCKTAIL

A rich and tart martini

————

London Dry Gin, Marseille Dry Vermouth, Maraschino Liqueur, Orange Bitters

> 2 dashes House Orange Bitters (page 234)
> ¼ ounce Luxardo Maraschino liqueur
> 1 ounce Noilly Prat Extra Dry vermouth
> 2 ounces Beefeater gin
> Lemon twist, for garnish

Combine all the ingredients except the garnish in a mixing glass. Fill the
mixing glass with ice and stir. Strain the cocktail into a coupe. Express
the oils from the lemon twist over the glass, and insert it into the cocktail.

GLASS: Coupe   ICE: None

UP TO DATE

A lighter Manhattan with orange

Rye Whiskey, Orange Curaçao, Sherry, Angostura and Orange Bitters

    1 dash House Orange Bitters (page 234)
    4 dashes Angostura bitters
    ¼ ounce Lustau Los Arcos amontillado sherry
    ½ ounce Grand Marnier
    1 ounce Lustau East India Solera cream sherry
    1½ ounces Russell's Reserve 6-Year rye whiskey
    Lemon twist, for expressing

In a chilled mixing glass, combine all the ingredients except the lemon twist. Fill the mixing glass with 1¼-inch ice cubes and stir. Strain the cocktail into a chilled coupe. Express the oils of the lemon twist over the drink, then discard the twist.

GLASS: Coupe   ICE: None

VASQUEZ DAIQUIRI

A chocolaty daiquiri

Barbadian Rum, Crème de Cacao, Coffee Amaro, Lime

    ¼ ounce Cane Syrup (page 218)
    ¼ ounce Caffè Moka
    ¾ ounce Marie Brizard crème de cacao
    ¾ ounce lime juice
    1½ ounces Mount Gay Black Barrel rum

In a cocktail tin, combine all the ingredients. Fill the tin with 1¼-inch ice cubes. Cover and shake. Strain the cocktail into a chilled coupe.

GLASS: Coupe   ICE: None

WARD 8

A whiskey sour with orange and pomegranate

Bonded Rye Whiskey, Grenadine,
Lemon, Orange

½ ounce Grenadine (page 232)

½ ounce lemon juice

½ ounce orange juice

2 ounces Rittenhouse bonded
rye whiskey

Combine all the ingredients in a cocktail tin. Fill the tin with ice, cover, and shake. Strain the cocktail into a coupe.

GLASS: Coupe   ICE: None

ZOMBIE FOR TWO

A boozy tiki cocktail with passionfruit and anise

Rums, Velvet Falernum, Absinthe, Passionfruit, Lime, Grapefruit, Pineapple, Cinnamon, Angostura Bitters

6 dashes Angostura bitters
10 dashes Pernod Absinthe
Scant ½ ounce Ceylon Cinnamon Syrup (page 219)
½ ounce Passionfruit Syrup (page 240)
½ ounce grapefruit juice
½ ounce John D. Taylor's Velvet Falernum
½ ounce Plantation pineapple rum
½ ounce Hamilton 151 Demerara rum
¾ ounce Hamilton Jamaican gold rum
¾ ounce lime juice
1 ounce pineapple juice
1 ounce Santa Teresa 1796 rum
2 lime wheels, for garnish
2 lemon wheels, for garnish
2 orange half-wheels, for garnish
Pineapple top, for garnish

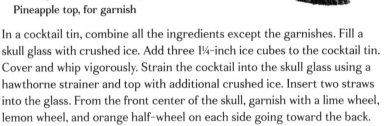

In a cocktail tin, combine all the ingredients except the garnishes. Fill a skull glass with crushed ice. Add three 1¼-inch ice cubes to the cocktail tin. Cover and whip vigorously. Strain the cocktail into the skull glass using a hawthorne strainer and top with additional crushed ice. Insert two straws into the glass. From the front center of the skull, garnish with a lime wheel, lemon wheel, and orange half-wheel on each side going toward the back. Place the pineapple top in the center back side of the skull.

GLASS: Skull or 16- to 18-ounce tiki mug   ICE: Crushed

SOFT
COCKTAILS

BASIL-FENNEL SODA

A refreshing highball with basil and fennel

Basil, Fennel, Lemon

½ ounce lime juice

1½ ounces lemon juice

1½ ounces Basil Fennel Syrup (page 217)

2 ounces Seagram's club soda

1 fennel frond, for garnish

Combine the lime and lemon juices and basil fennel syrup in a cocktail tin. Fill a highball glass with 1¼-inch ice cubes. Fill the tin with ice, cover, and shake. Strain the cocktail into the highball glass. Add the club soda and garnish with the fennel frond.

GLASS: Highball   ICE: 1¼-inch cubes   CREATOR: Leo Robitschek

BEET UP

An earthy sour with rich crème fraîche

Genmaicha Tea, Crème Fraîche, Beet, Cardamom, Lime, Grapefruit

2 lime wedges, for muddling
4 cardamom pods, for muddling
¼ ounce Agave Syrup (page 216)
1 ounce Genmaicha Crème Fraîche (page 230)
1 ounce grapefruit juice
½ ounce Seagram's club soda
½ ounce beet juice, to float

In a cocktail tin, muddle the lime wedges. Strain the lime juice into a jigger to measure ¼ ounce and then pour the juice back into the tin, discarding the rest. Add the cardamom pods to the tin and lightly muddle. Add the remaining ingredients except the club soda and beet juice. Fill a highball glass with crushed ice. Add three 1¼-inch cubes to the tin. Cover and shake. Add the club soda to the tin. Strain the cocktail into the highball glass. Add more crushed ice to the glass and float the beet juice on top.

GLASS: Highball   ICE: Crushed   CREATORS: Matthew Hunter and Pietro Collina

CEASE AND DESIST

Our take on a classic orange creamsicle

Orange Juice, Orange Blossom Water, Cream

1 ounce Simple Syrup (page 245)

1 ounce cream

3 ounces orange juice

2 ounces Seagram's club soda

5 drops orange blossom water

Combine the simple syrup, cream, and orange juice in a cocktail tin. Cover the tin and dry shake. Prime a fizz glass with 1 ounce of the club soda. Fill the tin with ice, cover again, and shake. Strain the cocktail into the fizz glass. Top with the orange blossom water and remaining club soda.

GLASS: Fizz   ICE: None   CREATOR: Leo Robitschek

DEVLIN'S DELIGHT

A coconut-ginger flip

Almond Milk, Ginger, Coconut

¾ ounce Coconut Syrup (page 225)

¾ ounce Spicy Ginger Syrup (page 247)

3 ounces Pacific Organic unsweetened almond milk

Grated lime zest, for garnish

Combine all the ingredients except the lime zest in a cocktail tin. Fill the tin with ice, cover, and shake. Strain the cocktail into a single rocks glass. Garnish with the lime zest.

GLASS: Single rocks   ICE: None   CREATOR: Eamon Rockey

DEVOCION TONIC

A bitter, citrusy coffee highball with grapefruit

Coffee, Grapefruit, Lemon, Vanilla

¼ ounce lemon juice
½ ounce Vanilla Syrup (page 249)
1 ounce grapefruit juice
1 ounce Cold Brew Coffee Concentrate (page 226)
2 ounces Fever-Tree tonic water
Grapefruit twist, for garnish

In a cocktail tin, combine all the ingredients except the tonic water and garnish. Fill a highball glass with 1¼-inch ice cubes. Fill the tin with 1¼-inch ice cubes. Cover and shake. Strain the cocktail into the highball glass using a hawthorne strainer and a fine tea strainer. Add the tonic water and garnish with the grapefruit twist.

GLASS: Highball   ICE: 1¼-inch cubes   CREATORS: Leo Robitschek and Guillermo Bravo

GINGERED ALE

Our take on ginger beer

Ginger, Lime, Turbinado

¾ ounce lime juice
¾ ounce Ginger Lime Syrup (page 231)
1½ ounces Spicy Ginger Syrup (page 247)
2 ounces Seagram's club soda
1 lime wedge, for garnish

Combine the lime juice, ginger lime syrup, and spicy ginger syrup in a cocktail tin. Fill a highball glass with 1¼-inch ice cubes. Fill the tin with ice, cover, and shake. Strain the cocktail into the highball glass and add the club soda. Garnish with the lime wedge.

GLASS: Highball   ICE: 1¼-inch cubes   CREATOR: Leo Robitschek

GOTHAM PARKSIDER

A maple–green tea refresher

Green Tea, Maple Syrup, Egg, Star Anise

1 egg
½ ounce Grade A maple syrup
2 ounces In Pursuit of Tea Jasmine Pearl green tea
Star anise, for garnish

Combine the egg, maple syrup, and tea in a cocktail tin. Cover the tin and dry shake to emulsify the egg. Fill the tin with ice, cover again, and shake. Strain the cocktail into a single rocks glass. Garnish with the star anise, grated with a Microplane.

GLASS: Single rocks   ICE: None   CREATOR: Leo Robitschek

GUIDARA'S SOBER MANHATTAN

A teetotaler's Manhattan

Seedlip Spice, Verjus, Maple Syrup, Coffee, Walnut Bitters

2 dashes Fee Brothers black walnut bitters

1 teaspoon Cold Brew Coffee Concentrate (page 226)

¼ ounce grade A maple syrup

Scant ½ ounce cherry juice

½ ounce Fusion verjus blanc juice

1½ ounces Seedlip Spice 94

Cherry, for garnish

In a mixing glass, combine all the ingredients except the garnish. Place a 2-inch ice cube and a cherry in a double rocks glass. Fill the mixing glass with 1¼-inch ice cubes and stir. Strain the cocktail into the rocks glass.

GLASS: Double rocks   ICE: 2-inch cube   CREATORS: Nathan O'Neill and Christina Thurston

LA PIÑA

A pineapple sour

———

Pineapple, Lime, Jalapeño, Agave

¾ ounce Jalapeño-Infused Agave Syrup (page 235)
¾ ounce lime juice
1 ounce pineapple juice
1 ounce Seagram's club soda

Combine all the ingredients except the club soda in a cocktail tin. Fill a fizz glass with 1¼-inch ice cubes. Fill the tin with ice, cover, and shake. Strain the cocktail into the fizz glass and top with the club soda.

GLASS: Fizz   ICE: 1¼-inch cubes   CREATOR: Jessica Gonzalez

OCHA

A yogurt drink with lime

———

Green Tea, Sheep's Milk Yogurt, Cinnamon, Lemon, Lime

Scant ½ ounce lemon juice
½ ounce lime juice
1 ounce Ceylon Cinnamon Syrup (page 219)
2 ounces Green Tea Yogurt Syrup (page 232)
1½ ounces Seagram's club soda
Lime zest, for garnish

In a cocktail tin, combine all the ingredients except the club soda and garnish. Fill the tin with 1¼-inch ice cubes. Cover and shake. Pour the club soda into the tin, then strain the cocktail into a fizz glass using a hawthorne strainer and fine tea strainer. Garnish with lime zest.

GLASS: Fizz   ICE: None   CREATOR: Leo Robitschek

PARADISE CITY

A tropical creamsicle

Grapefruit, Vanilla, Passionfruit, Cream

½ ounce Vanilla Syrup (page 249)
½ ounce Passionfruit Syrup (page 240)
1 ounce grapefruit juice
1 ounce cream
2 ounces Seagram's club soda
5 drops orange blossom water

In a cocktail tin, combine all the ingredients except the club soda and orange blossom water. Cover the tin and dry shake. Prime a fizz glass with 1 ounce of the club soda. Fill the cocktail tin with 1¼-inch ice cubes. Cover and shake again. Strain the cocktail into the fizz glass using a hawthorne strainer and fine tea strainer. Top with the orange blossom water and remaining 1 ounce club soda.

GLASS: Fizz   ICE: None   CREATOR: Leo Robitschek

PETER PIPER

A savory and tart pineapple cooler

Pineapple, Passionfruit, Lime, Black Pepper, White Balsamic Vinegar

2 lime wedges, plus lime juice as needed

10 dashes white balsamic vinegar

½ ounce Tellicherry Black Pepper Syrup (page 248)

½ ounce Passionfruit Syrup (page 240)

¾ ounce pineapple juice

1½ ounces Seagram's club soda

3 pineapple fronds, for garnish

Squeeze the lime wedges into a jigger and then fill the jigger with lime juice until you reach ½ ounce. In a cocktail tin, combine the lime juice, lime rinds, and remaining ingredients except the garnish. Fill a highball glass with crushed ice. Add three 1¼-inch ice cubes to the cocktail tin. Cover and whip. Strain the cocktail into the highball glass and top with additional crushed ice. Garnish with the pineapple fronds.

GLASS: Highball   ICE: Crushed   CREATOR: Pietro Collina

POLKA-MAN

A refreshing beverage with coffee and strawberries

———

Strawberry, Pineapple, Grapefruit, Vanilla, Lemon, Coffee, Tonic

    2 medium strawberries, 1 for muddling and 1 for garnish
    ¼ ounce Simple Syrup (page 245)
    ½ ounce Vanilla Syrup (page 249)
    ½ ounce Cold Brew Coffee Concentrate (page 226)
    ½ ounce lemon juice
    1 ounce grapefruit juice
    1 ounce pineapple juice
    1 ounce Fever-Tree tonic water

In a cocktail tin, muddle one of the strawberries. Add the remaining ingredients except the tonic water and garnish. Fill a highball glass with 1¼-inch ice cubes. Prime the highball glass with the tonic water. Fill the cocktail tin with 1¼-inch ice cubes. Cover and shake. Strain the cocktail into the highball glass. Garnish with the remaining strawberry.

GLASS: Highball   ICE: 1¼-inch cubes   CREATOR: Will Wyatt

SPRING AND TONIC

A nonalcoholic gin and tonic

———

Seedlip Garden, Grapefruit, Yuzu, Fennel, Tonic

   1 teaspoon yuzu juice
   ½ ounce Basil Fennel Syrup (page 217)
   ¾ ounce grapefruit juice
   1½ ounces Seedlip Garden 108
   2½ ounces Fever-Tree tonic water
   Lime wedge, for garnish

In a cocktail tin, combine all the ingredients except the tonic water and
garnish. Fill the tin with 1¼-inch ice cubes. Cover and shake. Strain the
cocktail into a fizz glass. Top with the tonic water and garnish with
the lime wedge.

GLASS: Fizz   ICE: None   CREATORS: Pietro Collina
                                        and Matthew Hunter

UP THE ALLEY

An apple and maple sour

———

Fuji Apple Cider, Sparkling Apple Cider, Lemon, Maple Syrup

   ½ ounce Grade A maple syrup
   ½ ounce lemon juice
   2 ounces Fuji apple cider
   1 ounce Duché de Longueville nonalcoholic sparkling cider
   1 orange twist, for garnish

Combine all the ingredients except the sparkling cider and orange twist
in a cocktail tin. Fill the tin with ice, cover, and shake. Strain the cocktail
into a coupe glass. Top with the sparkling cider. Flame the orange twist
over the drink, then discard the twist.

GLASS: Coupe   ICE: None   CREATOR: Eamon Rockey

YUZU ARNOLD PALMER

A floral and citrusy Arnold Palmer variation

Oolong Tea, Yuzu, Lemon

¼ ounce yuzu juice
¾ ounce lemon juice
¾ ounce Simple Syrup (page 245)
3 ounces Sunset Oolong Cold Brew (page 248)
2 ounces Seagram's club soda
Lemon wedge, for garnish

In a cocktail tin, combine all the ingredients except the club soda and garnish. Fill a highball glass with 1¼-inch ice cubes. Fill the tin with 1¼-inch ice cubes. Cover and shake. Strain the cocktail into the highball glass using a hawthorne strainer and a fine tea strainer. Top with the club soda and garnish with the lemon wedge.

GLASS: Highball   ICE: 1¼-inch cubes   CREATOR: Zach Ventura

BASICS

AGAVE SYRUP (2:1)

  650 g organic light blue agave nectar
  200 g hot water
  Brix: 50

Stir the agave into the hot water until it's fully dissolved. Let the syrup cool to room temperature and store in an airtight container, refrigerated, for up to 1 month.

MAKES 850 G

AVOCADO SYRUP

  525 mL filtered water
  945 g sugar
  945 mL lime juice
  945 g soft avocado flesh

In a medium bowl, combine the water and sugar and stir until dissolved. Add the lime juice and avocados, blend with an immersion blender until smooth, and then strain through a chinois. Store in an airtight container, refrigerated, for up to 2 days.

MAKES 3.8 L

BANANA OLOROSO

  1 L Lustau Oloroso Sherry
  4 overripe/black bananas, peeled
  4 mg Pectin X

Blend together the sherry, bananas, and pectin. Add to a Spinzall, 375 mL at a time, and put on continuous until the liquid becomes clear, then strain through a chinois. Store in an airtight container, refrigerated, for up to 1 month.

MAKES 1 L

BASIL FENNEL SYRUP (1:1)

100 g basil leaves
100 g fennel, roughly chopped
800 g Simple Syrup (page 245)
Brix: 48

Combine the basil, fennel, and simple syrup in an iSi canister. Charge it twice using N_2O (cream) chargers, shaking the canister between each charge. Allow the canister to sit for 5 minutes and then vent by pushing the nozzle out quickly; place a container underneath the tip to catch any liquid that may be released. Unscrew the top of the canister. Once the liquid stops bubbling, strain the mixture through cheesecloth or a coffee filter. Let the syrup cool to room temperature and store in an airtight container, refrigerated, for up to 1 month.

MAKES 800 G

BRANDIED CHERRIES

400 g sugar
475 g water
Peel of 2 navel oranges, excess pith (white part) removed
120 mL lemon juice
4 whole cinnamon sticks
4 whole star anise
6 vanilla beans, split
900 g Bing cherries, washed and pitted
475 mL Germain Robin brandy

Combine the sugar, water, orange peel, lemon juice, cinnamon, star anise, and vanilla beans in a large saucepan. Bring to a boil, then lower the heat to a simmer. Add the cherries and simmer until heated through. Remove the saucepan from the heat and stir in the brandy. Store the cherries and liquid in an airtight container in the fridge for 5 days before using; the cherries will continue to macerate and are optimal after 2 weeks. They will keep for up to 6 months.

MAKES 900 G

BROWN BUTTER FALERNUM

905 g unsalted butter, cubed
3 L John D. Taylor's Velvet Falernum

In a large pot over medium heat, melt the butter, whisking constantly, while the milk solids brown evenly. Continue to let brown, whisking, until the color is as dark as an almond skin. Remove from the heat and add the velvet falernum. Transfer the butter to a storage container and place in the freezer until the fat has risen to the top and solidified. Remove and discard the solidified fat cap. Store in an airtight container, refrigerated, for up to 1 month.

MAKES 3.5 L

CANE SYRUP (2:1)

500 g evaporated cane sugar
225 g hot water
Brix: 55

Stir the sugar into the hot water until it's fully dissolved. Let the syrup cool to room temperature and store in an airtight container, refrigerated, for up to 1 month.

MAKES 500 G

CASSIA CINNAMON SYRUP (1:1)

300 g cinnamon or cassia bark
800 g Simple Syrup (page 245)
Brix: 48

Muddle the cinnamon until it is broken up into shards. Combine the cinnamon and simple syrup in an iSi canister. Charge it twice using N_2O (cream) chargers, shaking the canister between each charge. Allow the canister to sit for 5 minutes and then vent by pushing the nozzle out quickly; place a container underneath the tip to catch any liquid that may be released. Unscrew the top of the canister. Once the liquid stops bubbling, strain the mixture through cheesecloth or a coffee filter. Let the syrup cool to room temperature and store in an airtight container, refrigerated, for up to 1 month.

MAKES 800 G

CELERY ROOT–INFUSED DOLIN DE CHAMBERY BLANC VERMOUTH

500 g celery root, peeled and diced
750 mL Dolin de Chambery Blanc vermouth

Preheat the oven to 200°C/400°F and line a sheet pan with parchment paper. Place the celery root on the prepared sheet pan and roast until dark golden brown, 25 to 30 minutes. In a large bowl, combine the celery root and vermouth, let steep for 1 hour, and then strain through a chinois. Store in an airtight container, refrigerated, for up to 8 weeks.

MAKES 750 ML

CEYLON CINNAMON SYRUP (1:1)

250 g Ceylon cinnamon sticks
800 g Simple Syrup (page 245)
Brix: 48

Muddle the cinnamon until it's broken up into shards. Combine the cinnamon and simple syrup in an iSi canister. Charge it twice using N_2O (cream) chargers, shaking the canister between each charge. Allow the canister to sit for 5 minutes and then vent by pushing the nozzle out quickly; place a container underneath the tip to catch any liquid that may be released. Unscrew the top of the canister. Once the liquid stops bubbling, strain the mixture through cheesecloth or a coffee filter. Let the syrup cool to room temperature and store in an airtight container, refrigerated, for up to 1 month.

MAKES 800 G

CHAI-INFUSED COCCHI VERMOUTH DI TORINO

30 g chai tea
750 mL Cocchi Vermouth di Torino

In a large bowl, combine the tea and vermouth, let steep for 3 to 5 minutes (taste as you go because it becomes tannic very quickly), and then strain through a chinois. Store in an airtight container, refrigerated, for up to 6 weeks.

MAKES 750 ML

CHAI-TURMERIC SYRUP

90 g chai tea
2.7 kg hot filtered water
2.7 kg sugar
3 g xanthan gum
30 g Arabic gum
15 g turmeric

In a large container, steep the tea in the hot water for 12 minutes. Pass the liquid through a chinois, but do not to press the loose tea, as the liquid will be bitter. Add the sugar and stir until fully dissolved, then transfer the mixture to a high-speed blender. While blending, sift in the xanthan gum, then the Arabic gum, and then the turmeric. Store in an airtight container, refrigerated, for up to 1 month.

MAKES 4 L

CHAI-TURMERIC YOGURT SYRUP

500 mL Chai-Turmeric Syrup (preceding recipe)
500 mL unsweetened sheep's milk yogurt

In a medium bowl, combine the syrup and yogurt and stir until fully incorporated. Store in an airtight container, refrigerated, for up to 1 month.

MAKES 1 L

CHAMOMILE HONEY SYRUP

25 g chamomile tea
225 g hot filtered water
350 g clover honey
Brix: 60

In a large container, steep the tea in the hot water for 3 minutes. Pass the liquid through a chinois, but do not to press the loose tea, as the liquid will be bitter. Add the honey and stir until fully dissolved. Let the syrup cool to room temperature. Store in an airtight container, refrigerated, for up to 1 month.

MAKES 575 G

CHARRED PINEAPPLE SYRUP

8 pineapples, peeled, cored, and sliced into 1-inch planks
Demerara Simple Syrup (page 227), as needed
Plantation pineapple rum, as needed

On a stove-top plancha or griddle, char the pineapple planks until black on both sides. Transfer the pineapple to an ovenproof container, cover with ovenproof plastic wrap, and place the container in a metal sheet pan. Steam in the combi oven for 30 minutes at 70°C/158°F and 100 percent humidity. Transfer the contents to a high-speed blender and slowly blend until completely smooth, then strain through a chinois. Combine 1 part demerara syrup and 1 part pineapple rum to 2 parts pineapple juice. Store in an airtight container, refrigerated, for up to 2 weeks.

CHICKEN JUS

100 g canola oil
560 g diced onions (2 cm)
260 g peeled and diced carrots (2 cm)
260 g diced celery (2 cm)
100 g tomato paste
750 mL red wine
4.5 kg chicken wings
2.5 kg chicken feet
13.5 kg water
2 bay leaves
10 thyme sprigs
25 black peppercorns

Preheat a convection oven to 200°C/400°F, with the fan on high. In a large roasting pan over high heat, warm the canola oil. Add the onions, carrots, and celery and sauté until they caramelize, about 12 minutes. Add the tomato paste and sauté until caramelized, 3 minutes more. Add the red wine and reduce by half, about 10 minutes, then set aside. Spread the chicken wings in a single layer on two large rimmed baking sheets and roast in the oven until caramelized, about 50 minutes, rotating the pan once. Drain and discard any rendered fat. Scrape the roasted wings into a large stockpot and add the chicken feet and water. Bring to a simmer over medium heat, skimming the stock of all impurities and fats that rise to the top. Add the vegetable mixture to the stock, along with the bay leaves, thyme, and peppercorns. Turn the heat to low and simmer, uncovered, for 6 hours, skimming every 30 minutes. Strain the stock through a chinois, transfer to a large clean saucepan, and continue to reduce over low heat until it is 1 kg. Strain the reduced jus through a chinois and chill over an ice bath. Store in an airtight container, refrigerated, for up to 3 days or freeze for up to 1 month.

MAKES 1 KG

CHOCOLATE SHELL

1 kg Pate a Glacer
500 g 70% dark chocolate
350 g grapeseed oil

Fill a medium pot three-fourths full with water and bring to boil. Lower the heat to maintain a simmer. In a large mixing bowl, combine the Pate a Glacer, chocolate, and grapeseed oil and place over the simmering water; be sure the bowl doesn't touch the water. Using a rubber spatula, stir continuously until the mixture is melted and completely combined. Store in an airtight container, refrigerated, for up to 1 month.

MAKES 1.9 L

CACAO NIB–INFUSED PIERRE FERRAND 1840 COGNAC

150 g cacao nibs
750 mL Pierre Ferrand 1840 Cognac

Combine the cacao nibs and Cognac in an iSi canister. Charge it twice using N_2O (cream) chargers, shaking the canister between each charge. Allow the canister to sit for 5 minutes and then vent by pushing the nozzle out quickly; place a container underneath the tip to catch any liquid that may be released. Unscrew the top of the canister. Once the liquid stops bubbling, strain the mixture through cheesecloth or a coffee filter. Store in an airtight container, refrigerated, for up to 1 month.

MAKES 750 ML

COCONUT-INFUSED ABSOLUT ELYX

150 g shredded coconut
750 mL Absolut Elyx vodka

Combine the coconut and vodka in a bag and vacuum seal. Steam in the combi oven for 30 minutes at 60°C/140°F and 100 percent humidity, then strain through a chinois. Transfer to a storage container and place in the freezer until the fat has risen to the top and solidified. Remove and discard the solidified fat cap and strain the vodka through muslin. Store in an airtight container, refrigerated, indefinitely.

MAKES 750 ML

COCONUT-INFUSED MICHTER'S BOURBON

150 g shredded coconut
750 mL Michter's Straight Bourbon

Combine the coconut and bourbon in a bag and vacuum seal. Steam in the combi oven for 30 minutes at 60°C/140°F and 100 percent humidity, then strain through a chinois. Transfer to a storage container and place in the freezer until the fat has risen to the top and solidified. Remove and discard the solidified fat cap and strain the bourbon through muslin. Store in an airtight container, refrigerated, indefinitely.

MAKES 750 ML

COCONUT SYRUP

200 g coconut chips, toasted
200 g coconut milk
200 g demerara sugar
Brix: 50

Toast the coconut chips for 5 minutes at 175°C/350°F, then transfer the chips to a bowl. Warm the coconut milk in a saucepan over medium heat until it's just below simmering. Remove from the heat and pour it over the coconut chips. Cover the mixture with plastic wrap and allow it to sit at room temperature for 30 minutes. Strain the mixture through a chinois or a superbag, pressing the coconut chips to extract all of the coconut milk. Add the sugar and mix until completely dissolved. Let the syrup cool to room temperature and store in an airtight container, refrigerated, for up to 1 month.

MAKES 400 G

COFFEE-INFUSED ANGOSTURA BITTERS

250 mL Cold Brew Coffee Concentrate (page 226)
250 mL Angostura bitters

In a medium bowl, combine the coffee concentrate and Angostura bitters and stir until fully incorporated. Store in an airtight container, refrigerated, for up to 1 month.

MAKES 500 ML

COFFEE-INFUSED DRY VERMOUTH

50 g whole coffee beans
500 mL Noilly Prat Extra Dry vermouth

Crush the coffee beans in a spice mill or coffee grinder until very coarsely ground. Put them into an iSi canister. Add the vermouth and seal the canister. Charge it twice using N_2O (cream) chargers, shaking the canister between each charge. Allow the canister to sit for 5 minutes and then vent by squeezing the nozzle quickly; place a container underneath the tip to catch any liquid that may be released. Unscrew the top of the canister. Once the liquid stops bubbling, strain the mixture through cheesecloth or a coffee filter. Let the liquid cool to room temperature and store in an airtight container, refrigerated, for up to 1 month.

MAKES 500 ML

COLD BREW COFFEE CONCENTRATE

455 g whole coffee beans, ground to medium coarseness
using a burr grinder
2 kg water

Place the ground coffee in a toddy or a ball jar, add the water, and stir gently until all of the grounds are submerged. Be careful to not overstir, or it will become overextracted. Cover and allow it to sit in the refrigerator for 18 hours. Strain through a coffee filter or cheesecloth. Store in an airtight container, refrigerated, for up to 1 week.

MAKES 1.8 KG

CORN SYRUP

2.7 kg freeze-dried corn
2.8 kg sugar
3.8 L hot water
Salt

In a high-speed blender, blitz the corn into a powder. Stir the sugar into the corn and add the hot water. Let steep for 15 minutes, then strain through a chinois and season with salt. Store in an airtight container, refrigerated, for up to 2 weeks.

MAKES 3.8 TO 4.7 L

CRANBERRY SYRUP

2 kg frozen cranberries
2 kg cranberry juice
500 g demerara sugar
Brix: 50

In a large saucepan, combine the cranberries and cranberry juice and bring to a boil over high heat. Lower the heat and simmer until all of the cranberries have popped. Remove the saucepan from the heat and let it sit for 10 minutes. Strain the mixture through a chinois and cheesecloth or through a superbag. Add the sugar and stir until fully dissolved. Let the syrup cool to room temperature and store in an airtight container, refrigerated, for up to 1 month.

MAKES 1 KG

DEMERARA SIMPLE SYRUP (1:1)

225 g demerara sugar
225 g hot water
Brix: 50

Stir the sugar into the hot water until it's fully dissolved. Let the syrup cool to room temperature and store in an airtight container, refrigerated, for up to 1 month.

MAKES 450 G

DILL SYRUP

150 g fresh dill
800 g Simple Syrup (page 245)
Brix: 48

Add the dill and simple syrup to an iSi canister. Charge it twice using N₂O (cream) chargers, shaking the canister between each charge. Allow the canister to sit for 5 minutes and then vent by squeezing the nozzle quickly; place a container underneath the tip to catch any liquid that may be released. Unscrew the top of the canister. Once the liquid stops bubbling, strain the mixture through cheesecloth or a coffee filter. Let the syrup cool to room temperature and store in an airtight container, refrigerated, for up to 1 month.

MAKES 800 G

EARL GREY SYRUP (1:1)

25 g In Pursuit of Tea Earl Grey tea
900 g hot water
800 g sugar
Brix: 48

Steep the tea in the hot water for 3 minutes. Strain the tea and add the sugar, stirring until it's fully dissolved. Let the syrup cool to room temperature and store in an airtight container, refrigerated, for up to 1 month.

MAKES 1.7 KG

EARL GREY–MILK WASHED
EXCELLIA BLANCO TEQUILA

25 g Earl Grey tea
750 mL Excellia Blanco tequila
15 mL lemon juice
100 mL milk

In an airtight jar, combine the tea and tequila, let steep for 20 minutes, and then strain. In a medium saucepan over medium heat, combine the lemon juice and milk and let simmer (do not boil) so the milk starts to curdle. Pour the curdled mixture into the infused tequila, whisk well, and then let sit for 30 minutes. Strain the mixture through a superbag or a coffee filter. Store in airtight container, refrigerated, for up to 2 months.

MAKES 750 ML

EUCALYPTUS BAY LEAF SYRUP

5 fresh bay leaves
1 L hot filtered water
1 kg sugar
1 g eucalyptus oil

In a large container, steep the bay leaves in the hot water for 5 minutes. Add the sugar and stir until fully dissolved. Stir in the eucalyptus oil (it is very potent, be sure to weigh it precisely). Pass through a chinois and let cool to room temperature. Store in an airtight container, refrigerated, for up to 1 month.

MAKES 1.5 L

FIG LEAF SYRUP

75 g fresh fig leaves
900 mL hot water
800 g sugar
Brix: 50

Rinse the fig leaves thoroughly under cool running water until the water runs clear, then remove the stems and tear up the leaves. Steep the leaves and hot water in a container for 10 to 15 minutes (taste as you go because it becomes bitter very quickly). Strain through a chinois and stir in the sugar until it dissolves. Store in an airtight container, refrigerated, for up to 1 month.

MAKES 1.4 L

GARDENIA SYRUP

1.8 kg clover honey
1.8 kg unsalted butter, cubed
140 g allspice dram
140 g Vanilla Syrup (page 249)
310 g Ceylon Cinnamon Syrup (page 219)

In a medium saucepan over medium heat, warm the honey until it starts to become liquid. (Be sure it does not get too hot or it will thicken.) Add the butter and whisk until it is melted and the mixture is smooth. Let sit for 5 minutes, then whisk in the dram, vanilla syrup, and cinnamon syrup and let cool. Store in an airtight container, refrigerated, for up to 4 weeks.

MAKES 2 L

GENMAICHA CRÈME FRAÎCHE

500 mL Green Tea Syrup (page 232)
500 mL crème fraîche

In a medium bowl, combine tea syrup and crème fraîche and stir until fully incorporated. Store in an airtight container, refrigerated, for up to 1 month.

MAKES 1 L

GINGER LIME SYRUP

600 g water
800 g light brown sugar
300 g ginger, chopped
20 g lime zest
95 g lime juice
Brix: 50

In a medium saucepan over medium heat, combine the water, brown sugar, and ginger and simmer for 45 minutes, stirring occasionally. Remove from the heat and add the lime zest. Allow to steep for 30 minutes. Strain out the ginger and lime zest and add the lime juice. Let the syrup cool to room temperature and store in an airtight container, refrigerated, for up to 1 month.

MAKES 1.5 KG

GRAPEFRUIT OLEO SACCHARUM

500 g grapefruit peels
500 g sugar
Brix: 60

Combine the grapefruit peels and sugar in a bag and vacuum seal, making sure that the peels and sugar are evenly distributed throughout the bag. Store at room temperature for 1 week. The sugar should absorb all of the oils of the grapefruit peels and have a syruplike consistency. If the sugar is still in granulated form, massage the bag and allow it to sit for another day. Strain the mixture and discard the peels. Store the syrup in an airtight container, refrigerated, for up to 1 month.

MAKES 600 G

GREEN TEA SYRUP

90 g Genmaicha green tea
2.7 kg hot water
800 g sugar
3 g xanthan gum
30 g Arabic gum

In a large container, steep the tea in the hot water for 12 minutes. Pass the liquid through a chinois, but do not to press the loose tea, as the liquid will be bitter. Add the sugar and stir until fully dissolved, then transfer the mixture to a high-speed blender. While blending at medium speed, sift in the xanthan gum and then the Arabic gum. Store in an airtight container, refrigerated, for up to 1 month..

MAKES 3.8 L

GREEN TEA YOGURT SYRUP

500 mL Green Tea Syrup (preceding recipe)
500 mL unsweetened sheep's milk yogurt

In a medium bowl, combine the tea syrup and yogurt and stir until fully incorporated. Store in an airtight container, refrigerated, for up to 1 month.

MAKES 1 L

GRENADINE

500 g R.W. Knudsen organic pomegranate juice
450 g turbinado sugar or Sugar In The Raw
225 g Cortas pomegranate molasses
10 orange twists
Brix: 55

Warm the pomegranate juice and sugar in a saucepan over medium heat. Stir until the sugar completely dissolves, making sure to never bring the juice to a boil. Remove from the heat and add the pomegranate molasses. Express the oils of the orange twists into the mixture and stir. Let the syrup cool to room temperature and store in an airtight container, refrigerated, for up to 2 weeks.

MAKES 1.1 KG

GUAVA SYRUP

1 L filtered water
2 kg guava puree
Sugar as needed
Brix: 50

In a medium container, whisk together the water and guava puree.
Stir in the sugar to taste. Store in an airtight container, refrigerated,
for up to 2 weeks.

MAKES 4.7 L

HONEY SYRUP (2:1)

350 g clover honey
225 g hot water
Brix: 60

Stir the honey into the hot water until it's fully integrated. Let the syrup
cool to room temperature and store in an airtight container, refrigerated,
for up to 1 month.

MAKES 575 G

HORSERADISH-INFUSED GIN

150 g horseradish, washed, peeled, and sliced lengthwise
750 mL Plymouth gin

Combine the horseradish and gin in a bag and vacuum seal. Steam in
the combi oven for 30 minutes at 60°C/140°F and 100 percent humidity,
then strain through a chinois. Store in an airtight container, refrigerated,
for up to 6 weeks.

MAKES 750 ML

HORSERADISH TINCTURE

150 g horseradish, washed, peeled, and diced
750 mL Absolut vodka

In a large bowl, combine the horseradish and vodka and let steep for 10 minutes, then strain through a chinois. Store in an airtight container at room temperature indefinitely.

MAKES 750 ML

HOT CHOCOLATE BASE

1.8 kg cream
200 g water
2 g salt
4 vanilla beans, split
150 g sugar
200 g 55 percent chocolate
260 g 72 percent chocolate

In a medium saucepan, combine the cream and water. Over medium heat, bring the mixture to just below a simmer, then remove the saucepan from the heat. Whisk in the salt, vanilla beans, sugar, and both chocolates. Let the mixture cool to room temperature and store in an airtight container, refrigerated, for up to 1 month.

MAKES 2.6 KG

HOUSE ORANGE BITTERS

200 g Angostura orange bitters
200 g Regans' orange bitters No. 6

Combine both ingredients and stir. Store in an airtight container at room temperature indefinitely.

MAKES 400 G

JALAPEÑO-INFUSED AGAVE SYRUP (2:1)

3 medium jalapeños
250 g hot water
810 g organic light blue agave nectar

Dice the jalapeños, retaining all the seeds, and steep in the hot water for 3 minutes. Taste the mixture to ensure that the spice level is to your taste. Allow them to steep longer for a spicier end product. Strain out the jalapeños when the desired spice level has been reached and stir the agave nectar into the jalapeño-infused water until it's fully integrated. Let the syrup cool to room temperature and store in an airtight container, refrigerated, for up to 1 month.

MAKES 1.1 KG

JALAPEÑO-INFUSED TEQUILA

5 medium jalapeños, diced
750 ml Excellia Blanco tequila

Steep the jalapeños and tequila in a container for 5 minutes. Taste the mixture to ensure that the spice level is to your taste. Allow to steep longer for a spicier end product. Strain out the jalapeños when the desired spice level has been reached. Store in an airtight container, refrigerated, indefinitely.

MAKES 750 ML

JASMINE PEARL SYRUP (1:1)

32 g In Pursuit of Tea Jasmine Pearl green tea
900 g hot water
800 g sugar
Brix: 48

Steep the tea in the hot water for 3 minutes. Strain the tea and add the sugar, stirring until it's fully dissolved. Let the syrup cool to room temperature and store in an airtight container, refrigerated, for up to 1 month.

MAKES 1.7 KG

KABOCHA SQUASH SYRUP (1:1)

800 g Kabocha Squash Water (following recipe)
800 g demerara sugar
Brix: 50

In a saucepan over medium heat, heat the squash water until it's simmering. Remove from the heat and stir the sugar into the water until fully dissolved. Let the syrup cool to room temperature and store in an airtight container, refrigerated, for up to 1 month.

MAKES 1.6 KG

KABOCHA SQUASH WATER

1 kabocha squash, quartered and seeded
1.6 kg water
6 g salt
15 g whole allspice
100 g Ceylon cinnamon sticks, crushed

Preheat the oven to 200°C/400°F. Place the squash on a sheet pan and roast for 1½ hours. When cool enough to handle, scoop out the flesh of the squash, discarding the rest. Measure out 900 g of the roasted squash and add to a saucepan along with the water, salt, allspice, and cinnamon. Boil over high heat for 10 minutes. Strain the mixture though a chinois. Let the water cool to room temperature and store in an airtight container, refrigerated, for up to 1 week.

MAKES 1 KG

LAPSANG SOUCHONG–INFUSED DE KUYPER CRÈME DE CACAO

30 g Lapsang Souchong black tea
1 L De Kuyper crème de cacao

Combine the tea and crème de cacao in a container and let steep for 45 minutes, then strain the mixture through a chinois. Store in an airtight container, refrigerated, indefinitely.

MAKES 1 L

LAVENDER-INFUSED HONEY SYRUP (2:1)

10 g dried lavender flowers
350 g clover honey
225 g hot water
Brix: 60

Stir the lavender flowers and honey into the hot water until the honey is
fully dissolved. Let the syrup cool to room temperature and store in an
airtight container, refrigerated, for up to 1 month.

MAKES 575 G

LEMON VERBENA–INFUSED BUTTERMILK

500 mL Lemon Verbena Syrup (following recipe)
500 mL buttermilk

In a medium bowl, combine the syrup and buttermilk and stir until
fully incorporated. Store in an airtight container, refrigerated, for
up to 1 month.

MAKES 1 L

LEMON VERBENA SYRUP (1:1)

32 g dried lemon verbena
900 g hot water
800 g sugar
Brix: 48

Steep the lemon verbena in the hot water for 5 minutes. Strain the
mixture and stir in the sugar until it's fully dissolved. Let the syrup cool
to room temperature and store in an airtight container, refrigerated,
for up to 1 month.

MAKES 1.7 KG

MINT-INFUSED BOURBON

35 g mint leaves
750 mL Old Forester 86 bourbon

Combine the mint and bourbon in an iSi canister. Charge it twice using
N_2O (cream) chargers, shaking the canister between each charge. Allow
the canister to sit for 5 minutes and then vent by pushing the nozzle
out quickly; place a container underneath the tip to catch any liquid that
may be released. Unscrew the top of the canister. Once the liquid stops
bubbling, strain the mixture through cheesecloth or a coffee filter. Store
in an airtight container, refrigerated, indefinitely.

MAKES 750 ML

MUSHROOM BROTH

100 g dried shiitake mushrooms
1 L hot water

In a large bowl, combine the mushrooms and hot water and let steep for
30 minutes. Strain the mixture through a coffee filter and let come to
room temperature. Store in an airtight container, refrigerated, for up
to 1 week.

MAKES 1 L

MUSTARD SEED-INFUSED KIKORI WHISKEY

40 g horseradish, washed, peeled, and chopped
100 g ground mustard seeds
750 mL Kikori whiskey

Combine the horseradish, mustard seeds, and whiskey in an iSi canister.
Charge it twice using N_2O (cream) chargers, shaking the canister between
each charge. Allow the canister to sit for 5 minutes and then vent by
pushing the nozzle out quickly; place a container beneath the tip to catch
any liquid that may be released. Unscrew the top of the canister. Once
the liquid stops bubbling, strain the mixture through a chinois. Store in
an airtight container, refrigerated, for up to 8 weeks.

MAKES 750 ML

OLIVE OIL–WASHED TEQUILA

30 g extra-virgin olive oil
750 mL Excellia Blanco tequila

Combine the olive oil and tequila in an airtight jar. Every 30 minutes, shake the jar for about 15 seconds. After 3 hours, put the jar in the freezer for 8 hours. Skim any solids off the top and strain the mixture through a coffee filter. Store in an airtight container, refrigerated, for up to 2 months.

MAKES 750 ML

OOLONG SYRUP

30 g Wood Dragon oolong tea
950 g hot water
800 g sugar
Brix: 50

Steep the oolong tea and hot water in a container for 12 minutes. Taste to ensure that the mixture is to your liking. Strain through a chinois (do not press or the tea will become too tannic) and then stir in the sugar until it is dissolved. Store in an airtight container, refrigerated, for up to 1 month.

MAKES 1.9 L

ORGEAT

500 g sliced almonds
800 g water
800 g sugar
20 drops orange blossom water
Brix: 50

Preheat the oven to 100°C/200°F. Spread the almonds on a sheet pan and toast until lightly golden, about 20 minutes. Crush the almonds using a food processor. Transfer to a large container and add the water. Allow to sit for 8 hours. Strain the mixture through cheesecloth into a bowl, squeezing the cheesecloth to extract all the liquid. Add the sugar and orange blossom water and stir until the sugar is dissolved. Let cool to room temperature and store in an airtight container, refrigerated, for up to 1 month.

MAKES 1.6 KG

PANDAN-INFUSED JOHNNIE WALKER BLACK LABEL SCOTCH

2 pandan leaves
750 mL Johnnie Walker Black Label Scotch

Combine the pandan leaves and Scotch in a bag and vacuum seal.
Steam in the combi oven for 30 minutes at 70°C/160°F and 100 percent
humidity, then strain through a chinois. Store in an airtight container,
refrigerated, indefinitely.

MAKES 750 ML

PASSIONFRUIT SYRUP

1 kg passionfruit puree
300 g sugar
Brix: 50

In a medium bowl, stir together the passionfruit puree and sugar until fully
incorporated. Store in an airtight container, refrigerated, for up to 1 month.

MAKES 1.3 KG

PINEAPPLE GOMME

800 g Simple Syrup (page 245)
200 g diced pineapple
Brix: 48

Combine the simple syrup and pineapple in an iSi canister. Charge it
twice using N_2O (cream) chargers, shaking the canister between each
charge. Allow the canister to sit for 5 minutes and then vent by pushing
the nozzle out quickly; place a container underneath the tip to catch
any liquid that may be released. Unscrew the top of the canister. Once
the liquid stops bubbling, strain the mixture through cheesecloth or a
coffee filter. Let the syrup cool to room temperature and store in an
airtight container, refrigerated, for up to 1 month.

MAKES 800 G

PURPLE CORN SYRUP

1 cinnamon stick
2 whole cloves
Skin of ½ pineapple, washed
455 g dried purple corn
2.84 kg filtered water
Sugar as needed
Brix: 50

In a large pot over high heat, combine the cinnamon, cloves, pineapple skin, corn, and water and bring to a boil. Cover the pot with aluminum foil and let simmer for 45 minutes; the corn kernels will start to crack open. Strain the mixture through a chinois and then stir in sugar to taste. Store in an airtight container, refrigerated, for up to 1 month.

MAKES 4.7 L

RAISIN-INFUSED BARBANCOURT BLANC RHUM

100 g raisins
1 L Barbancourt Blanc Rhum

Combine the raisins and rhum in a bag and vacuum seal. Steam in the combi oven for 15 minutes at 60°C/140°F and 100 percent humidity, then strain through a chinois. Store in an airtight container, refrigerated, indefinitely.

MAKES 1 L

RASPBERRY CONSOMMÉ

300 g raspberries

Vacuum seal the raspberries in a plastic bag, then place in a combi oven. Cook at 100°C/200°F for 1 hour with 100 percent humidity. Build a three-tier pan apparatus with a bottom catch pan, medium perforated pan, and top pan, then line the perforated pan with cheesecloth. Lay the raspberries in the perforated pan and wrap with the cheesecloth. Place the top pan on top of the wrapped raspberries, then add a 4.5- to 9-kg weight to the top pan. Allow it to sit overnight in a refrigerator.

MAKES 225 G

RASPBERRY SYRUP (1:1)

200 g sugar
225 g Raspberry Consommé (preceding recipe)
Brix: 48

Stir the sugar into the raspberry consommé until it is fully dissolved. Let the syrup cool to room temperature and store in an airtight container, refrigerated, for up to 2 weeks.

MAKES 425 G

RED BELL PEPPER AND THAI BIRD CHILE–INFUSED BAROLO CHINATO

4 Thai bird chiles, chopped
2 red bell peppers, seeded and chopped
1 L Cocchi Barolo Chinato

Combine the chiles, bell peppers, and chinato in an iSi canister. Charge it twice using N_2O (cream) chargers, shaking the canister between each charge. Allow the canister to sit for 5 minutes and then vent by pushing the nozzle out quickly; place a container underneath the tip to catch any liquid that may be released. Unscrew the top of the canister. Once the liquid stops bubbling, strain the mixture through cheesecloth or a coffee filter. Store in an airtight container, refrigerated, for up to 1 month.

MAKES 1 L

RED PEPPER AGAVE SYRUP

475 mL red pepper juice
945 mL Agave Syrup (page 216)

In a large bowl, combine the red pepper juice and agave syrup and stir
until fully incorporated. Store in an airtight container, refrigerated, for
up to 2 weeks.

MAKES 1.4 L

RED PEPPER HONEY SYRUP

475 mL red pepper juice
2.7 kg clover honey

In a large bowl, combine the red pepper juice and honey and stir until
fully incorporated. Store in an airtight container, refrigerated, for up
to 2 weeks.

MAKES 1.4 L

RHUBARB SHRUB

40 g salt
200 g sugar
1 kg white balsamic vinegar
1.02 kg water
950 g rhubarb, washed and cut into 1-inch pieces
5 drops red food coloring

In a large bowl, combine the salt, sugar, vinegar, and water and stir to
make a brine. Combine the brine and rhubarb in a bag and vacuum seal.
Place the bag in a sheet pan and steam in the combi oven for 15 minutes at
63°C/145°F and 100 percent humidity. Transfer the bag to the refrigerator
and let chill, then strain the liquid through a chinois and stir in the food
coloring. Store in an airtight container, refrigerated, indefinitely.

MAKES 2.5 L

RHUBARB SYRUP (1:1)

250 g rhubarb juice
250 g demerara sugar
Brix: 50

To make the juice, run whole stalks of rhubarb through an auger or
masticating juicer. Strain the juice through a chinois. Warm the juice in
a medium saucepan over medium heat until it's just under a simmer. Add
the sugar and stir to dissolve. Let the syrup cool to room temperature
and store in an airtight container, refrigerated, for up to 2 weeks.

MAKES 500 G

ROASTED POBLANO PEPPERS

1 teaspoon olive oil
3 large poblano peppers

Preheat the broiler and line a baking sheet with parchment paper. Rub
the olive oil all over the poblanos, then place the peppers on the prepared
baking sheet. Roast until the peppers' skin is charred, turning them four
times, about 8 minutes total. Remove from the oven and let cool to
room temperature, then peel and seed the peppers. Store in an airtight
container, refrigerated, for up to 1 week.

MAKES ABOUT 225 G

ROASTED POBLANO PEPPER SYRUP

500 g Roasted Poblano Peppers (preceding recipe)
250 g water
300 g sugar
Brix: 50

In a high-speed blender, combine the roasted peppers and water and
process to a smooth, even consistency. Pass through a chinois and then
stir in the sugar. Store in an airtight container, refrigerated, for up to
2 weeks.

MAKES 500 ML

SALINE SOLUTION

50 g kosher salt
500 mL warm water

In a large bowl, combine the salt and water and stir until the salt is fully dissolved. Store in an airtight container, refrigerated, indefinitely.

MAKES 500 ML

SARSAPARILLA TINCTURE

500 g neutral alcohol, such as vodka or Everclear
250 g dried sarsaparilla root

Combine the alcohol and sarsaparilla in an airtight container and allow it to sit at room temperature for 10 days. Don't allow the tincture to steep for too long, as it will become increasingly woody, tannic, and astringent. Strain through a chinois and store in an airtight container at room temperature indefinitely.

MAKES 500 G

SIMPLE SYRUP (1:1)

200 g sugar
225 g hot water
Brix: 48

Stir the sugar into the hot water until it is fully dissolved. Let the syrup cool to room temperature and store in an airtight container, refrigerated, for up to 1 month.

MAKES 425 G

SORREL-INFUSED DOLIN DE CHAMBERY BLANC VERMOUTH

100 g sorrel
750 mL Dolin Blanc vermouth

Blend the sorrel and vermouth together using a high-speed blender. Strain the liquid, add it to a bag, and seal using a cryovac. Place the bag into a water bath with an immersion circulator that has been preheated to 60°C/145°F. Remove the bag after 30 minutes and place it in a water bath until it reaches room temperature. Strain the vermouth through a coffee filter and store in an airtight container, refrigerated, for up to 2 months.

MAKES 750 ML

SPICED TOMATO WATER

2 medium jalapeños, seeded
8 stalks celery, diced
20 lemon thyme leaves
100 bay leaves
40 g grated horseradish
2 kg tomatoes, diced
Salt
80 g lemon verbena leaves
400 g lemon juice

Line the bottom of a perforated bucket with muslin and set over another clean container. In a large bowl, combine the jalapeños, celery, lemon thyme leaves, bay leaves, horseradish, tomatoes, and 30 g salt. Blend with an immersion blender until liquefied, then pour the mixture into the prepared bucket and let drain overnight. The next day, in a medium saucepan over medium heat, bring 900 mL of the liquid to simmer. Add the lemon verbena and let steep for 5 minutes. Stir in the remaining liquid and the lemon juice and season with salt, then strain through a chinois. Store in an airtight container, refrigerated, for up to 2 weeks.

MAKES 4 L

SPICY AVUA CACHAÇA

3 medium jalapeños, seeded and sliced into rings
750 mL Avua Prata cachaça

Steep the jalapeños and cachaça in a container for 15 minutes. Taste the mixture to ensure that the spice level is to your liking. Allow to steep longer for a spicier end product. Strain out the jalapeños when the desired spice level has been reached. Store in an airtight container, refrigerated, indefinitely.

MAKES 750 ML

SPICY GINGER SYRUP

250 g ginger juice
250 g turbinado sugar or Sugar In The Raw
Brix: 50

To make the juice, run whole stalks of ginger through an auger or masticating juicer. Strain the juice through a chinois and cheesecloth or through a superbag, straining out the lighter colored starches that remain on the bottom of the container. Warm the juice in a medium saucepan over medium heat until it's just under a simmer. Add the sugar and stir to dissolve. Let the syrup cool to room temperature and store in an airtight container, refrigerated, for up to 2 weeks.

MAKES 500 G

STRAWBERRY PICKLING LIQUID

500 g white balsamic vinegar
100 g sugar
20 g salt
510 g water
10 hulled strawberries

Combine all the ingredients except the strawberries in a saucepan and bring to a boil. Place the strawberries in a heatproof bowl, then pour the boiling liquid over the top. Allow the mix to cool to room temperature, then store in an airtight container, refrigerated, for up to 1 month.

MAKES 450 G

SUNSET OOLONG COLD BREW

8 g Rare Tea Company Sunset Oolong Tea
1 L cold filtered water

Combine the tea and water and stir to mix. Loosely cover, let steep
in the refrigerator for 12 hours, and then strain. Store in an airtight
container, refrigerated, for up to 2 weeks.

MAKES 1 L

SZECHUAN PEPPERCORN–INFUSED GIN

100 g Szechuan peppercorns
1 L Plymouth gin

Steep the peppercorns and gin in a container for 30 minutes. Taste the
mixture to ensure that the spice level is to your liking. Allow to steep
longer for a spicier end product. Strain out the peppercorns when the
desired spice level has been reached. Store in an airtight container,
refrigerated, indefinitely.

MAKES 1 L

TELLICHERRY BLACK PEPPER SYRUP

150 g Tellicherry black pepper, coarsely ground
800 g Demerara Simple Syrup (page 227)

Combine the pepper and simple syrup in an iSi canister. Charge it twice
using N_2O (cream) chargers, shaking the canister between each charge.
Allow the canister to sit for 5 minutes and then vent by pushing the nozzle
out quickly; place a container underneath the tip to catch any liquid that
may be released. Unscrew the top of the canister. Once the liquid stops
bubbling, strain the mixture through cheesecloth or a coffee filter. Store
in an airtight container, refrigerated, for up to 1 month.

MAKES 800 G

THAI BIRD CHILE–INFUSED APEROL

10 Thai bird chiles, diced
750 mL Aperol

Steep the chiles and Aperol in a container for 5 minutes. Taste the mixture to ensure that the spice level is to your liking. Allow to steep longer for a spicier end product. Strain out the chiles when the desired spice level has been reached. Store in an airtight container, refrigerated, indefinitely.

MAKES 750 ML

VANILLA SYRUP

800 g Simple Syrup (page 245)
3 vanilla beans, split

Combine the simple syrup and vanilla in an iSi canister. Charge it twice using N_2O (cream) chargers, shaking the canister between each charge. Allow the canister to sit for 5 minutes and then vent by pushing the nozzle out quickly; place a container underneath the tip to catch any liquid that may be released. Unscrew the top of the canister. Once the liquid stops bubbling, strain the mixture through cheesecloth or a coffee filter. Store in an airtight container, refrigerated, for up to 1 month.

MAKES 800 G

WHEY SYRUP

900 mL yogurt whey
800 g sugar
Brix: 50

In a large bowl, combine the whey and sugar and blend with an immersion blender until fully incorporated. Strain the mixture through a chinois. Store in an airtight container, refrigerated, for up to 2 weeks.

MAKES 1.9 L

MAI TAI COCKTAIL EXPLOSION

A tart, classic rum tiki cocktail with almonds

Aged Guyanese Rum, Aged Jamaican Rum, Overproof Agricole Rum, Orange Liqueur, Orgeat, Lime

SERVES 15

4 lime twists

4 ounces Clément Créole Shrubb Liqueur d'Orange

4 ounces Rhum J.M Blanc Agricole Martinique 100 Proof rum

6 ounces Orgeat (page 239)

6 ounces Appleton V/X Jamaican rum

6 ounces El Dorado 15-Year rum

8 ounces lime juice

15 mint leaves, for garnish

20 lime wheels, for garnish

20 mint plouches, for garnish

Divide all the ingredients except the garnishes among two cocktail tins. Line the bottom of an explosion vessel with the mint leaves, then fill halfway with crushed ice. Line the inside of the vessel with 10 of the lime wheels, tucking them into the crushed ice, making sure they touch but do not overlap. Fill the explosion vessel to the top with crushed ice. Line the rim with the remaining 10 lime wheels, again tucking them into the crushed ice. Add three 1¼-inch ice cubes to each tin. Cover and whip. Strain the cocktails into the explosion vessel and top with additional crushed ice. Garnish with the mint plouches around the top of the ice.

GLASS: Explosion vessel   ICE: Crushed

ABOUT THE AUTHOR

Managing Partner and Bar Director Leo Robitschek has been with the Make It Nice team since 2005 and played a significant role in the development of the group's cocktail program at both Eleven Madison Park and The NoMad locations in New York, Los Angeles, and Las Vegas.

A native of Venezuela, Leo first began working in hospitality while attending the University of Miami, but it was upon moving to New York City that his appreciation for the craft of cocktails began to come into focus. After joining Eleven Madison Park in 2005, he helped reinvent the cocktail program of the restaurant and was promoted to head bartender in 2009. With an approach that stressed balance, the best ingredients, and technique, the cocktail program echoed the same high standards as those of Chef Daniel Humm's kitchen.

Since opening NoMad New York in 2012, Leo and his team have been the recipients of numerous Tales of the Cocktail Foundation Spirited Awards as well as the James Beard Award for Outstanding Bar Program, have been consistently ranked on the prestigious World's 50 Best Bar List, and named the Best Bar in North America.

ABOUT THE ILLUSTRATOR

Antoine Ricardou is the founder of Le Studio be-pôles, a boutique design studio based in Paris and New York, which started in 2000. Be-pôles's work ranges from publishing projects, product design, and brand architecture to logo and illustrative work. Antoine is responsible for the graphic identity of The NoMad Hotel and the bespoke art program for each of the hotel's guest rooms and dining rooms.

ACKNOWLEDGMENTS

Thanks to Chef Daniel Humm and Will Guidara, who helped me shape a career and much more. In the years since I first walked into Eleven Madison Park, I've built an incredible family, found my identity, and created a life that brings me joy every day. Thank you for believing in me, even during moments when I doubted myself. You've taught me that as individuals we can achieve greatness, but as a team we can accomplish the impossible.

To Jeff Tascarella, the other managing partner and my partner all things NoMad, I couldn't have gotten through the expansion and last few years without you. Thank you for making me laugh and for questioning everything we do. You make the machine run and make us better in every way.

To Andrew Zobler, Sydell, our partners at MGM . . . you are the best. Thank you for collaborating with us and supporting our crazy visions.

Aaron Ginsberg had the hard job of corralling me—getting me to sit still and to focus on only one task—and endured the punishment of drinking with me. Thank you.

Emily Timberlake, Julie Bennett, and Doug Ogan of Ten Speed Press, your combined patience and expertise allowed me to write something intelligible. Thank you for understanding my vision, providing ingenious solutions, and allowing me to have a voice.

To Pietro Collina, my loyal right-hand man and travel partner, your attention to detail and pursuit of excellence have helped The NoMad become what it is today, and without you, our expansion couldn't be possible and would be missing a spark and a bit of flair.

To Nathan McCarley-O'Neill, our incredibly talented, hardworking, and inspiring East Coast bar director, your tenacity ensures that we will always be better today than we were yesterday, although sometimes your Irish brogue makes it impossible to understand you. Thank you for elevating the team, dreaming big, and your willingness to join me on this journey, no matter how impossible it may seem. I know you'll always keep running ahead of the pack.

To David Purcell, Adam George Fournier, David Bonatesta, Ivonne Moy, and Josh Ben-Yaish, you've made our expansions possible with your ideas, originality, hard work, blood, sweat, laughs, and tears.

To Matt Hunter and Jim Betz, two parts of EMP's strong backbone and our local curmudgeons, without your impossible standards, I couldn't have opened The NoMad in the first place. Thank you for making me look good.

To Laura Wagstaff, Kristen Millar, Sarah Rosenberg, and Katy Foley, my favorite ladies, thank you for being my emotional support.

To the barbacks of The NoMad—past, present, and future—some of the hardest-working ladies and gentlemen; the bar team would be lost without you.

Billy Peelle III, our bar ambassador and director of operations, we love you so much that we named a cocktail after you.

To HQ, thank you for doing the tireless work that makes all of our lives better.

To Michael Smoley, LJ Sconzo, Shaun Dunn, Michelle Jackson, Noah Friedman, Julia Reingold, Tyler Caffall, Matt Chavez, Gianna Johns, you are the glue that holds The NoMad together. Thank you for being such badasses.

To the bartenders of The NoMad—past, present, and future—in my eyes, you're the best bar team in the world, and I couldn't be more honored to work alongside you.

To the leaders of The NoMad, in both the dining room and the kitchen, who push boundaries, readily embrace collaboration, and meet every challenge we face head-on.

To our culinary development team and pastry team, thank you for sharing your knowledge.

To my family—Mom, Dads (Jose and Danny), Raquel, Tamara, Gloria, Kassandra, and Arianna: Thank you for being supportive even when you disagreed with all my decisions. You taught me to work hard and never give up, to listen and not be afraid to have a voice. Knowing that you will always be there to pick me up when I fall has allowed me to be brave and to take risks. I love you all.

INDEX

Published in the United States by Ten Speed Press, an imprint of
Random House, a division of Penguin Random House LLC, New York.
www.tenspeed.com

Ten Speed Press and the Ten Speed Press colophon are registered
trademarks of Penguin Random House LLC.

Portions of this material appeared in *The NoMad Cookbook*, published
in 2015 by Ten Speed Press, an imprint of Random House, a division of
Penguin Random House LLC.

Library of Congress Cataloging-in-Publication Data is on file with
the publisher.

Hardcover ISBN: 978-0-399-58269-1
eBook ISBN: 978-0-399-58270-7

Printed in China

Design by be-pôles

10 9 8 7 6 5 4 3 2 1